The Scrap-Paper Miracle

Don Madaris

New Hope

Birmingham, Alabama

New Hope
P. O. Box 12065
Birmingham, Alabama 35202-2065

©1993 by New Hope
All rights reserved. First printing 1993
Printed in the United States of America

Dewey Decimal Classification: 248.24
Subject Headings: FAITH
 CONVERSION—PERSONAL NARRATIVE
 PRISONERS—PERSONAL NARRATIVE
 PRISON MINISTRIES

Cover design by Barry Graham

N934111•0193•5M1
ISBN: 1-56309-022-8

Contents

Foreword v
How It All Came to Be vii
Chapter 1: His Last Day to Live 1
Chapter 2: Pots, Pans, Tortillas, and Wildflowers 6
Chapter 3: August 11—A Scrap of Hope 11
Chapter 4: Tell Me About Your God 18
Chapter 5: Postmark: Penjamo Jail 22
Chapter 6: Your Sins Will Find You Out 26
Chapter 7: Like Sheep Without a Shepherd 31
Chapter 8: That Gideon New Testament 37
Chapter 9: No One Cares About Me 41
Chapter 10: Peace, Pardon, and Joy 47
Chapter 11: The Family of God 51
Chapter 12: A New Creation 56
Chapter 13: The Road to Penjamo 60
Chapter 14: That We Might Learn 66
Chapter 15: My Grace Is Sufficient 73
Epilogue—What's Happened Since 78

Foreword

In 1987 on a missions trip through Central America, I sat in the lovely Guadalajara, Mexico, home of missionaries Don and Kay Madaris. I had met them several years earlier in Richmond, Virginia. At that time they had delighted me with the wonderful story of their romance.

We recalled some of the details they had shared with me in Richmond: Kay had been serving as a missionary nurse at the Baptist hospital in Guadalajara for 16 years. Don (a bachelor) had come to Mexico on a Volunteers in Missions assignment for the Foreign Mission Board (FMB) of the Southern Baptist Convention. One evening his missionary host arranged a tennis foursome which included this lovely single nurse named Kay. Beginning that day, "love" was more than a score. At the end of his assignment, Don returned to the States; a long-distance courtship followed. In the unfolding of time, Don felt God's call to the missions field in general and Guadalajara in particular; and their love grew. Kay returned to the US; they married; Don took his required seminary hours; he was appointed a career missionary by the FMB; she, reappointed; and they returned to Guadalajara together.

As we visited that day in 1987, Don, by then a chaplain assigned to the American Mexican Hospital in Guadalajara, began to tell me another wonderful story. Before he finished, I knew I wanted Rudolfo Halcon's experiences shared with others, for they reinforced many truths important to missions-hearted people.

I was interested in all aspects of his account. However, one factor stood out—the role of prayer in Rudolfo's experiences. There was no evangelical church or witness within miles of the remote town of Penjamo. How could a scrap of paper from Bible study material published in El Paso, Texas, have reached that far? Why did Rudolfo happen to read it? Why did the few words he read, but failed to understand, strike such a soothing and responsive chord in his desperate, depressed, and suicical life? Was it coincidence that the author's name and the address of the publishing house appeared on that scrap paper? There is no logical explanation; it is one of God's miracles. Later Rudolfo became convinced the prayers of God's people for the lost of the world caused that scrap paper to blow into the jailhouse courtyard, grab his attention, and stir his soul as he swept and cleaned the area.

The story shows the significance of prayer at every point. From the moment Olivia S. D. Lerin, author of the words on the scrap paper, received Rudolfo's letter, she bathed him in prayer and enlisted others to do so. Diminutive and dynamic, she was one of the giants among Baptist women of Latin America, a woman of earnest, daily, extraordinary prayer. As she answered his questions with words of care and assurance about God's love and forgiveness, she prayed for God to prepare Rudolfo's heart for the reading of her letter. She wrote missionary James Crane in Guadalajara and the pastor of First Baptist Church, Guadalajara, to involve these men in Rudolfo's life. A prayer group of missionaries in Guadalajara entered into a serious prayer relationship with Ruldolfo and his family. A group of Baptist women in Juárez, Mexico, "adopted" the Halcons. A Baptist Women prayer group in New Mexico prayed consistently for them. Many sources of witness, ministry, and discipleship developed over the months and years; none so essential as the prayers lifted for Rudolfo and his family.

As Don concluded the story, he told of Rudolfo's repeated request that believers be urged to pray for the lost of the world, even though they have no way of knowing names, faces, or locations. Does God honor such "general" prayers? Rudolfo believes He does—and so do I! Simply, but profoundly, Rudolfo's story illustrates and reinforces this truth.

After you have read this book, I urge you to pass it on. On second thought, you will not need my urging. You too will want to share this compelling miracle.

Minette Drumwright
Foreign Mission Board

How It All Came to Be

For several years now, I have carried the following account around in my mind with the fullest intentions of writing it down. To simply say it's the story of a Mexican man and his family just does not say all I need to say.

I first heard parts of his story during a missionary prayer meeting in Guadalajara, Mexico, way back in the spring of 1979. How I came to be in Guadalajara during that particular spring is another whole story in itself. Let me just say that I was on an assignment as a Volunteer in Missions with the Foreign Mission Board of the Southern Baptist Convention. I was assigned there to work with students at the Baptist student center in that large city. Each Monday I looked forward to the afternoon prayer and sharing time always held in one of the missionary's homes.

It was on just such an afternoon as this that Kay Weldon, who had been working as a missionary nurse at the Mexican American Hospital for 16 years, shared briefly about a visit she and some friends from El Paso had made the weekend before. Her sharing set in motion the beginning thoughts of this book. Allow me to publicly thank her for a simple prayer request that inspired this written account.

Very slowly the information made its way onto paper. I felt the story deserved to be told, but for a long time I felt very, very unqualified to try to write it. I at least wrote a brief account of the prayer request in my journal in order to retain something of the spiritual excitement of it all. But each time I tried to write more, I discovered what those writers much more experienced than I have come to call writer's block. I thought I knew what I wanted to say and I had certain ideas of how I wanted to say it, but it just never seemed to fall into place as I thought it should.

Some months after I wrote the first outline for the book, I discovered something important. It is something many people know, but I think it comes to each of us in different ways. *I* had been trying to write all of this. *I* knew what *I* wanted to say. And *I* had certain ideas of how *I* wanted to say it. The Lord had other ideas, however. After some time of "struggling along in my dead-end way," I gave this project to Him. From that day until now, He has filled my mind with the words and guided my hands as I wrote them down. He has helped me write and rewrite and publish this book. I give Him all the thanks and any praise which may come from all of this.

Now, after all of that, let me say there is also another very human reason for the years which have passed during the writing. It has taken some time for me to put all the facts together and get them into a readable order. I started doing that while in Mexico, continued in the United States, then traveled back to Mexico, then back to the States, and I am now completing the writing back in Mexico. The story contains some minor freedoms of poetic license—which is a writer's way of saying that the events may not have happened *exactly* the way they are written here.

That admission does not change the fact that this is a true story which happened to real people. Some of the names and locations have been changed for obvious reasons; but, hopefully, none of that will change the message which I trust will reach your heart and life.

During the years since I began writing all of this, I have read and reread the manuscript many times. Each time I discover that I am greatly challenged by the original message there—not the message written by this writer, but that one shared by a man who by his own admission never thought his own life would make a difference to anyone. His is a message of hope and endurance and trust in the Lord. It's the message of a saving Christ as told through the man's life and struggles and those of his wife and children. May God somehow touch your life in a new way as you read and experience this true-life spiritual adventure.

Don Madaris

1
His Last Day to Live

Rudolfo Halcon did not want to live to see the sunrise of another day. He had been a prisoner in the city jail of Penjamo for over two years. In all this time he had never seen a lawyer. His case had never even been brought to court.

Rudolfo was tired. All this waiting had made him tired in body, spirit, and soul. People were beginning to repeat promises he had heard before. He was weary of listening to so many empty promises.

Bored of repeating each worthless day, frustrated by life, tired of having to live it in the same endless and monotonous way, he decided he had not done a very good job with the life he had been given. Maybe he could at least do something good by bringing it to an end. If he had his way, this would be his last day to live.

Penjamo was just one of dozens of small-time, look-alike towns in south central Mexico. It was not small in population. It just looked that way. It was located off the main highway, which completely bypassed the town. That alone said a great deal about Penjamo. It had been passed by for a long time. Its winding streets—some rough cobblestone, some dirt, some mud—passed stores and houses and schools; but like most of these out-of-the-way Mexican towns, the road narrowed to one lane before it came to the center of town where it circled the plaza. There is one consistent thing about all Mexican towns. Even if it has little else, it always has a plaza.

In the center of this plaza was the traditional bandstand surrounded by trees and sidewalks, fountains, and flower gardens. Lining the sidewalks were a dozen or two concrete benches.

One of the mental images many people have of Mexico is of the siesta hour when dusty, tired workers sit slumped against trees, floppy-brimmed sombreros pulled down over their faces while they sleep for an hour or two. It is not really a bad stereotypical image, but it is not true. Most of the time, the Penjamo plaza benches were filled by people resting from a walk around the plaza or a tiring trip to the market. Sometimes the benches were full of mothers watching their children chase the pigeons that stay around for the last crusty piece of tortilla. Sometimes lovers sat on the benches stealing late-afternoon kisses. At other times, the benches were full of those tired old men taking their afternoon siestas.

Rudolfo thought of the many times when he had enjoyed resting there in the shade enjoying the cool breeze, listening to the music amid the beauty of the flowers. But that was before his arrest. Now he was just across the street behind the strong steel gate of the municipal jail.

He had been long lost in thought, but was rudely interrupted by a loud knocking. He called out from his daydreams, "Socorro! Socorro!" The voice of the prison guard at the gate brought him back to reality when he yelled back, "Hey, Rudolfo, nobody's looking for you! Nobody!"

Even though the person knocking was not looking for him, it sent his mind racing back to that particular day when, because of a knock on their door, his wife and children first learned of his arrest. His wife, Socorro, had described that day in such vivid detail that he could not get it out of his mind. Even when he tried to clear his mind of other things, this scene was still there, as vividly as Socorro had told it. Once again he relived it. How could he ever forgive himself for what had happened to them that particular afternoon many months ago?

Socorro had been busy in the kitchen preparing the afternoon meal. There was a loud pounding at the front door.

"Ruth," she called out, "could you get the door, please? If it's one of your friends, tell her you can visit with her later. For now, it's almost time to eat. And after that call your sister and brothers. They need to get ready too." Socorro went on with what she was doing as she waited for the children to gather.

The Halcon children were named Rudolfo, Socorro, Ruth, and Daniel. Rudolfo, named for his father, was 13. Socorro, named for her mother, was 10. Ruth was 8 and little Daniel was only 5. The older three had only recently come in from school, where they had classes in the mornings. Because of the many, many boys and girls in Mexico who want to go to school, there is a divided schedule for classes. One group of children attends classes in the mornings and is free in the afternoons. Others are free during the morning and attend school during the afternoon.

The Halcon children liked their schedule for they were able to be home for the family meal each afternoon. Many times their father did not get to eat with them. He was studying too, or else he was busy doing his own work away from the house. Today they hoped he was coming home from his out-of-town business trip, and they were busily helping get things ready for the meal.

Socorro was right in the middle of completing a tortilla. She had finally gotten it just right and was about to drop it on the ones already on the griddle when she heard the front door open. The sound of the door opening was immediately followed by a terrifying scream from little Ruth. Socorro dropped the tortilla. She turned just in time to see some strange men rudely pushing little Ruth and Daniel through the archway that led from the living room into the kitchen. She could tell by the way they were dressed that they were important men. She could also tell by the way they moved that they were not very polite men.

They had obviously come there with something to do, and whatever it was did not appear to be too pleasant. Without any warning or explanation, she and the children were almost bodily thrown out of the house. The men talked continuously to each other in loud voices as if Socorro and the children did not even exist; or at least it did not seem to matter that they heard what the men were saying.

"Just start right here with that table by the door," one man shouted to the other one. "Just haul everything out to the truck. Try not to break it up or get things too scratched up. It looks to me like it might bring a pretty peso on the open market."

The other man began to bark orders as well. "Don't forget the clothes. Or the drapes. And the mirrors. And the paintings. From the looks of this place, I'd say they lived pretty well!"

The first one answered, "Yeah. Now come on, let's get to work." And with that, the men began taking all the furnishings and personal belongings out of the house and put them into a large truck.

The children screamed and cried and Socorro was too shocked to ask many questions. She tried talking to the men, but they had other things on their minds. She did somehow manage to ask why they were doing all of this. As one of the men pushed her out of his way, he grunted, "It's all because of your husband."

"My husband? Where is he? What's happened to him? What has he done?"

The children took up the questions. "What have you done with our father? Where is our father?" they begged to know. "Please tell us," they shouted through their tears.

The men did not even have the decency to answer their questions. With a cruelty Socorro had never known before, the men took even the rings and bracelets she and the girls were wearing. The little Halcon family stood by and watched until almost everything they had was loaded into the truck.

Socorro told her children to stay where they were—huddled together under the trees on one side of the house. While the men were loading one of the last loads into the truck, she ran into the house through the back door. The stack of tortillas had been brushed aside. She quickly wrapped them in a shawl that had been dropped in one corner of the bedroom. A few clothes lay in one of the children's closets. She threw them over her arm. With her free hand she picked up a few books which had been overlooked at the back of the bookcase. This was all she could carry. This was all the time she had. From the pots and pans scattered on the kitchen floor, she quickly picked up a couple. After all, she had no idea where they would have to eat their next meal. She put all these things under a bush at the back of the house and rejoined the children. Her timing was exactly right, for at that very moment one of the men came around the house shouting, "Now give me the keys to your car."

"I'll give them to you if only you'll tell me what's happened to my husband," she answered.

"No deal, Señora. Just give me the car keys."

She had no choice as he drew back his hand to slap her. She retrieved them from the pocket of her dress.

As the truck drove away, followed by the car, the man yelled out the window, "Your husband's in Penjamo in the city jail. That's all I can tell you. And that's all you need to know."

2
Pots, Pans, Tortillas, and Wildflowers

During the two and one-half years of being in the city jail, Rudolfo had relived that scene many times. Before his arrest he often left home in the morning with the loving memory of his wife and children standing there at the door waving to him until he was completely out of their sight. How many times that scene had reminded him of the love and support of those closest to him. How often it had given him the courage to keep going on when times were hard or when it seemed there was little use to try to make life worth living.

For all those months in jail, he had another memory of his little family standing outside their house. It was not as lovely a memory as that one where they were waving good-bye to him as he left home each day. His jail-cell memory was that painful one he had just brought to mind of them standing outside their house with tears running down their cheeks and with helpless, confused, and defenseless looks on their faces.

He had let them down. He had really let them down. He knew it. He also knew there was very little he could do about it now. It seemed there was nothing left for him to do but end his miserable life. He had thought so before, but now he was sure of it. Tonight would be the time. And for the first time in a long time he felt he could actually go through with it.

He had thought it through many times before. He had planned it over and over in his mind. He had never gone through with it before, but this time he felt nothing could stop him. Nothing. Or no one!

Sitting in the corner of his small cell Rudolfo could not contain all the frustration he felt. As a matter of fact, viewing the cell from that *rincon* (little corner) was contributing to his feelings of frustration in a very specific way. The cot with its bunched up mattress and one dirty serape for a spread only reminded him of the fine hand-carved furniture he had owned. A lot of it had been made by his very own hands with wood he had personally selected and bought.

The small folding table at the end of the bed, heavily loaded down with his personal items and food scraps, was a constant reminder that his wife and four children now lived like beggars, crowded together in one corner room of a condemned building in this remote little Mexican village.

There was a single nail in the cell wall on which he hung his change of clothes, consisting of a long-sleeved white shirt and another pair of dark trousers. Just looking at those things sent his memory tumbling backward to that time when he kept his clothes in that other closet in his well-equipped house, a closet loaded with the best clothes and shoes money could buy.

Rudolfo could not hold his deep-seated feelings of disgust and despair any longer. He could not look anyone in the face anymore. He was a failure. He was a public disgrace to all who knew him. And he had brought disgrace on his family. Furthermore, it seemed he had no hope of ever getting out of jail.

There were times in these lonely months when he seriously thought about breaking out. Many a night he lay on his cot looking up at the thin tile roof thinking to himself, It wouldn't take too much effort to get out of here. I could just put my chair on the table, pull up to the rafters, and just remove some of the tiles. After all, if this roof is like most of the roofs in Mexico, the tiles are probably just stacked there with one overlapping the other to keep out the rain. It would take just a minute and I could be over the wall and lost in the city before anyone ever knew I was gone. Why don't I do it then?

It was a useless question, for he knew the reason well. The reason was his dear family. Even if he were to get out, he knew he would always be a fugitive, and they would always be on the run. He could not subject them to that. He had convinced himself that his family would be better off without him.

The more he thought about it, the more he felt his new decision was a good one. It was a good one, and it was a right one, and it was an easy one—just to end it all. That very night! But there were several hours until the slowly fading sunset allowed the night to cover the jail. Until then, he found he could do nothing but think—think and remember how much his family had suffered because of him. Socorro had not told him about all that happened to them to make him suffer; but each time he thought of that day when his personal possessions had been hauled away in a truck and his wife and children were locked out of their house, it brought a new kind of torture to his mind.

It seemed that after the men drove away from the house with the truck full of their household goods, Socorro and her little ones found themselves just standing there outside staring off into the distance. They could not go back into the house, for the last thing the men did was to lock and seal all the doors and windows.

None of them understood why it had happened or what was going on, but there was nothing they could do. Socorro did her best to comfort and console the children, although at the moment she was beside herself with grief and confusion. The children would be looking to her for strength and comfort. No matter how she felt right now, she simply could not let her own fear and confusion be heard in her voice. As calmly as possible, she called out to them.

"Rudolfo, Socorro, Ruth, Daniel, come gather around me. There's something I need to say. Now, I don't know exactly what we're going to do, but there's one thing I know we're *not* going to do. If Papa were here with us, I'm sure he'd tell you the same thing. Since Papa's not here, you'll just have to depend on me. Now, we're not going to worry. It's easy to say, but I know it won't be easy to do; but we're going to try, aren't we?"

She waited for what seemed a long time until she saw some sign of affirmation in their eyes. Then she continued.

"Now, Rudolfo, take Daniel with you and go around to the back of the house. Look under the bougainvillea. You'll see some things I put there. Bring them here. Go on now. And hurry back. There are some other things we have to do."

After the boys left, she turned to the girls, still standing there wide-eyed and still. Pulling them close to her, she said, "I'm sure there's been some kind of mistake. Once they realize it is all a mistake, I'm sure they'll return all our things, and we'll be able to move back into our beautiful home again. For now, I don't know where we'll live, or where we'll go. But we have one thing for sure—we have each other. And we have to somehow find out where Papa is and let him know we're all right. If he *is* in the Penjamo jail as the men told us he was, I'm sure that's something of a mistake as well. If he's there, then we too have to somehow get to Penjamo. I know that all of this is frightening. It's a little scary to me too. But for now, go and see what's keeping those brothers of yours."

As the girls disappeared around the corner of the house, she could hardly keep her own mind from being flooded with questions. Had she been alone at this moment, she would have broken down; but for the sake of the children she could not do that.

It was one thing to tell them not to worry. It was quite another to keep herself from doing so. How could all this have happened? What would they do now? What had he done that was so bad? Where would they live? And even if they could get to Penjamo, how would they feed a family of five? Would she be able to get a job there? How would they live? She didn't know. Perhaps, worse than that, it seemed that at this very moment they were so alone. It seemed that no one cared about them. Her mind was racing now, trying to make some sense out of all of this.

Penjamo? she thought. Why? Penjamo's just a small village. What could Rudolfo possibly have done that would cause them to put him in jail? And even if they had to put him in jail, why did they take away everything we owned? And again, she could not help but feel a little sorry for herself and her family and think, No one seems to care about us. No one!

Her lonely thoughts were interrupted by the children, who came running around the house. Rudolfo was carrying one of the pans, inside of which were the tortillas still wrapped in the shawl. Socorro had some of the clothes over one arm and the other pot in the other hand. Daniel had one arm full of clothes and the books. Little Ruth trailed along behind with the remaining clothes in one hand. In the other hand, she held a large bunch of purple wildflowers, freshly picked near the bush where Socorro had hidden the only things they owned right now. She bit her lip and lovingly held them out to her mother, smiling at her with an innocent smile.

The tears welled up in Socorro Halcon's eyes. She didn't really know which to do first, hug the children or take the flowers. She tried to do both at the same time. But her thoughts were a long way away—in Penjamo, at the city jail.

3
August 11—A Scrap of Hope

Night finally came to Penjamo. It settled over the jail like a thick handwoven serape, leaving not so much as a seam of light. The moon would be along later to illuminate the deed which by moonrise would be finished. Rudolfo had been waiting for the night. He had finally made it through the long afternoon. He got his razor and towel. He wanted everything to look as normal as possible.

Just one little cut on the jugular and my life will just flow away—quietly, quickly. And as my lifeblood flows away, so will all the problems of this life. I'll put an end to this miserable existence. I'm sick of prison life, sick of the way I'm being forced to live, he thought bitterly.

He took one last glance around the small and cluttered room which had become home for him. No, he thought, this place has never become home for me. It has simply replaced home. It has merely been a place to sit, a place to sleep, a place to think, a place to eat. I won't miss it any more than all the other places in which I have sat and thought and eaten and slept.

He made sure his few personal things were in order. After all, someone would likely have to come in and get them. He didn't want that to be a problem at all. Especially if that person happened to be his wife, Socorro. And if it were not she, he had no idea who it would be.

He walked across the small courtyard to the semienclosed shower area. At that time of night, he was sure everyone else was asleep. They were not. A fellow prisoner was there, down on his knees on the dirty concrete floor gagging and retching into the old toilet. Rudolfo quickly realized this was not the place or the time to end his life. He decided to just wash his face and go back across the yard.

The August night was crisp, and he could hardly stand the thought of going back into that dark, small corner of a cell. So he threw his serape around his shoulders and spent the rest of the night sitting on the cold stone step outside his cell door. He had an idea that the next night he'd be able to finish the job with the razor.

The Lord seemed to have another idea in mind for Rudolfo Halcon, although the next day God was the farthest thing from his mind. He had only one intention—that was to live out this new day in anticipation of the night and his appointment with death.

That appointment would already have been met if that man had not been sick at his stomach the night before.

Why? he wondered. Of all times, why last night? I finally work up the courage to take my life and there's someone in my way. Why should that happen to me?

Even though he did not know it yet, this was all in *el plan de Dios* for his life. The plan of God did not interest him, however. He only wanted to hurry this day along. Like the one before, it seemed to be passing too slowly. For most prisoners, all days are the same. For Rudolfo, they had seemed to be so up until now. Though he had not noticed it before, even the usual routine of prison life was a slowly passing one. If the intention of those in charge of jails was to make prisoners aware of certain, more enjoyable parts of life they had given up in the outside world, they were accomplishing their intention to the fullest.

Those jailed here were not allowed the privilege of sleeping late, but there was little reason to get up early. The space in the bathhouse was limited. Even the sink and the cracked mirrors were in great demand by men who still felt it important to shave before breakfast. Rudolfo had long ago decided to forego this part of his routine and do his shaving at night. That is why he knew no one would give him a second thought when later on he would leave his room with his razor and towel in hand.

As for breakfast, it was usually not worth the wait. The variety consisted in whether the tortillas were served hot or cold. It did not matter much, for they were served on the side of a plate which also held a spoonful of beans, an occasional egg, and once in a while a chunk of cheese. Most of the men just mixed it all together in rather typical Mexican style and scooped it up with the tortilla, washing it down with large gulps of strong Mexican coffee. After breakfast, as well as after all other meals, each person was responsible for washing his own plate, cup, and fork, which were then kept in his own cell until the next meal.

After breakfast, as he washed the blue-and-white-speckled tin plate, he caught a quick glimpse of his own reflection in it. It set him to thinking about life. Maybe that was all it was, just a reflection. That was all he could see of himself right now. And that was all he could feel. There was no meaning, no depth, no movement in any direction, and no reason to keep looking for any. It seemed he had no reason to keep going, except for the oncoming night. How he wanted to hasten the day away. But the more he tried to rush the night, the slower the sunset seemed to come.

Late afternoon finally arrived. He had only one thing left to do before the evening shadows began to creep across the small cluttered courtyard. Every prisoner was assigned a prison job to do. Rudolfo's daily task was simple enough. He only had to sweep the courtyard and pick up all the trash that had blown in during the day.

Anyone who casually noticed him walking across the litter-filled yard would think nothing of it, for he was performing his daily routine. There was very little about him that would call attention to himself. Like most of his fellow countrymen, he was slight of stature. A few extra pounds, aided by the good life he had known before prison and approaching middle age, settled comfortably around his stomach. His skin was light. His hair was just beginning to streak with gray. He spoke with a soft, gentlemanly voice. On this particular day no one noticed the slight smile on his face as he took the large brush broom and began to sweep.

The weather was cool and windy at this time of the year. Clouds hung low over the nearby mountains. It was the beginning of the annual rainy season, and during the first days of rainy season there was a downpour almost every afternoon. In just a little while that cool and windy sky would be filled with a torrent of water, turning the dry and dirty concrete courtyard into a small flowing river of swirling water. The scraps of paper and leaves and other debris would float on the first streams of water to the small drain and immediately create a clog, causing a backup of water in the courtyard.

There was only one small step that led into the rooms, and when the water backed up, it made a mess in every one of the rooms. It was easier to clean the courtyard and the drains before the rain than to mop and clean all the cells later. So his daily job was to get the scraps up before it rained. Most of the time, he picked them up and threw them in his garbage sack without giving them so much as a second thought. For some reason quite unknown to him, he began looking at every scrap of paper he picked up. Reading them slowed him down somewhat, but time was not important—he had nothing else to do but wait for the night to come.

In all his time in prison he could never recall a time when he gave a second thought to what he was sweeping up. He had never stopped to read the litter that swirled around his feet. The things he picked up to read today were no more than the usual advertisements, announcements, and a piece torn from the sports page of the morning paper. There was nothing of particular significance, no reason for the sudden urge to read every word of every piece of litter he found.

Then his eyes caught the words printed on one scrap of paper. They were unusual words, printed in large letters right in the middle of the paper. He mouthed them silently several times, trying to think why they should be of any importance to him. He found himself reading them out loud.

Standing there in the middle of the courtyard, his broom resting against his shoulder, he read, "Be thou faithful unto death." Faithful? Unto death? Why this idea about death just as he was about to find out for himself? And as for being faithful, to what did his life offer any sense of faithfulness? He leaned the broom against a tree and concentrated on what followed.

> "Be thou faithful unto death, and I will give thee a crown of life" (Rev. 2:10). The Apostle John gave this advice not only to the Christians of that time in which he lived, but also to the Christians of all times.

This touched something in his memory. He was really thinking now. The Apostle John. I seem to remember hearing about him in catechism class when I was just a boy. I didn't care a lot about what they were saying then, but I seem to remember that he was one of those who followed Christ around. John was one of those disciples closest to Him. He listened to Christ and walked with Him and tried to follow His advice and counsel. Then he wrote down all that he thought might be important for people to know and remember. Maybe he does know what he's saying. But it says here that this advice is to the Christians of all times. Christians? But who are they? What does being a Christian really mean?

This was not a page from the sacred Scriptures. It was only a small scrap of paper torn from some sort of magazine. The name of the writer was printed right under the title—Olivia S. D. de Lerin. Just what does she know about faith and death that I don't know? he questioned in his mind. She's just a human being like I am. She can't possibly know so much! Yet on the other side of that scrap of paper was her name again, and her address.

She must be someone pretty special, he thought. I wonder just who she really is? The paper said she was the director of the department of Bible studies at the Baptist Spanish Publishing House in El Paso, Texas.

Maybe I could write to her. No, I don't have time to write. I don't want to wait for an answer. I certainly don't want any Bible studies right now. I know exactly what I want to do. And that's the end of it!

And it might have been, except that he stuck the paper into his shirt pocket rather than in his garbage sack. And that *was* the end of it! For that moment at least.

He finished his job. The late-afternoon rains came and went. The later-afternoon meal of tortillas and beans was served. Night began to close in around the small town of Penjamo. Someone out in the tree-lined plaza was strumming a guitar and singing. As Rudolfo lay on his back on the cot, he again pulled that piece of paper from his pocket as he had done so many times since he found it. He felt a strange attachment to it. It was suddenly a very personal possession. It was something that was his alone. It had not seemed to belong to anyone else before. And he read it. Again. And again.

That same sentence, "Be thou faithful unto death, and I will give thee a crown of life," appeared later in the article. And it was talking about suffering, trials and tribulations, and prison: "Fear none of these things which thou shalt suffer: behold, the devil shall cast some of you into prison, that ye may be tried; and ye shall have tribulation . . . : be thou faithful."

The more he read it, the more he wondered if it was talking specifically about him. After all, he surely was suffering trials and tribulations, and he had been cast into prison. Was it possible that there really *was* some way he could have this hope? Could this Olivia S. D. de Lerin really help him?

He thought, As a prisoner, I know I have no right to direct any sort of questions to a religious lady like she must be. Why, I'm so low-down that I've even been just one step away from taking my own life. God can't be too concerned with me. And even if He is, what difference can that make? Why should I write to a woman in another country for advice? Even if He is, what could she do for me? But I'll never know if I don't ask. It's worth a try. What harm can it do?

He could not sleep that night. For almost the first time since he had been there, he was thinking of the sunrise and the next day. He was also thinking of writing that letter to Olivia S. D. de Lerin. The night before had been so dark, and he had felt so helpless. Suddenly there was a small light of hope. And there was a ray of joy.

He spent that night thinking about how blessed he was to have found something important. He thought of other times and other places. When he was a boy, he had spent a lot of time in church. By his own admission, it had not really made much difference in his life. Yet now, he was not so sure about that. He remembered hearing his own mother quote holy sayings. He was not sure whether they came from the Bible or merely from her own life. He remembered how she had helped the family to face hardships and disappointments.

Suddenly he found himself searching his mind for some bits and pieces of the Scriptures he had learned as a boy. Even though he did not recognize it as prayer, he began to repeat statements like, "Please help me to write this letter, and please let there be some way I can get some help for all that I'm feeling." He spent the entire night thinking about things like that. He began to compose that letter in his mind. He did not want all those important questions to get away from him.

4
Tell Me About Your God

As Rudolfo awoke he heard a chorus of birds singing in the trees that surrounded the park. The jail walls might keep the prisoners inside, but they could not keep the singing of the birds outside. How often as a boy he had wondered about the creation of such lovely sounds.

On a completely different note, dogs announced that the man who delivered the milk was coming down the street. It may have seemed picturesque to the tourists, but the milk was still delivered to the local residents by a man whose burro carried two large milk cans tied on either side of him. If you wanted milk, you met him in the street with your own jar or pitcher or can. He would dip into the large one on the burro and pour out what was needed at each house. Mixed in with the sound of the birds and the dogs and the burro's clip-clop were the crowing roosters as they made their own noisy announcement of the coming of the day in all the distant streets. The shrill but lovely voices of children could also be heard as their cries echoed from the nearby houses. Streetsweepers were hard at work cleaning debris from the sidewalks and streets. Their hand-tied brush brooms made a distinctive swishing and scraping sound as they swept down the cobblestone pavement.

All those things let him know it was morning, but he was bothered by not knowing exactly what time it was. Another thing that he was not absolutely sure of—whether all that was running through his mind was not the last memory of some dream he had just had.

After a few minutes, he was able to recall everything about the day before. The desire to write that letter was as real in the daylight as it had been the night before, and had nothing to do with a foolish dream. Of course, he had to get his hands on some paper and a pen. Maybe he would just wait until visiting day to write the letter. That way his wife could bring him what he needed. No, he did not want to wait that long. How could he get some paper? Or better yet, how could he get a typewriter?

He remembered seeing an old beaten-up typewriter in one of the front offices the day they brought him in. It looked like it had not been used for years. Maybe it was still there. And if it was, did it even work? And if it worked, would they let him use it? It couldn't hurt to ask. All they could say was no.

But they said, "Yes, you can use it." They were going to bring it to his cell. He had never known the guards to be so nice and obliging to the prisoners before. Maybe there was a God, and maybe He was already working some things out. While he waited, he found the scrap of paper and read those by now very familiar words, "Be thou faithful unto death."

Following his night of meditation, they really caused him to think now. It felt like a command from God written especially to him. He continued to compose that letter in his mind as he had been doing for most of the night. He had so many questions to ask: What does "be faithful" mean? Do you really know God? Could this God really have mercy even on me? Will you please tell me about this God?

His thoughts were momentarily interrupted by the guard bringing him the typewriter. He told him he could keep it in his cell for as long as he needed it. Nobody was using it in the front office and it might as well help someone. Along with the typewriter, he handed him several sheets of paper. Rudolfo knew that this guard would have to read his letter before it left the prison. He knew they would try to give him a hard time about it. But that was not as important to him now as it had been before.

At that moment, his mind was racing in several directions all at the same time. The cot had now become an important place to think. And for a change, he was not thinking about death. The table became his desk. For a change, he was not even griping about the beans and tortillas. His questions began to form themselves into words. And the words began to pour out onto the crisp blank piece of paper he had just rolled into the carriage of that old typewriter.

"Dear Señora Lerin." He began by telling her something about his past life. Even though he was not proud of it, he wanted her to know him well enough to help him. He told her how he had come to be in prison. His thoughts were forming into words almost faster than his fingers could type. Every now and then he had to stop, scratch off a mistake, and start again. He began to think it might be better if he just wrote it out first, then typed it. No, he needed to get it done while it was fresh on his mind. Besides, he knew how he was. If he waited, he might change his mind. So he wrote on!

He told her about how he had come to find that piece of paper in the prison courtyard just hours before he planned to end his life. He confessed to her that just reading the words on that scrap of paper had made even his worst thoughts seem better. He told her all about his life. He confessed to her a lot of his shame. The words he chose to use revealed much about his desperation and his desire to know about God. He asked her his questions about the meaning of the words *be faithful*. He asked about the possible grace that the Lord might offer to a person like him. He poured out his heart to her.

He ended his letter by saying, "And if you're not ashamed to write a prisoner, I beg you, please write and tell me about this God." With those words, the emotions that had been building up inside him since he found that paper the afternoon before burst loose as a torrent of tears accompanied by chest-rattling sobs. No one who heard him would have thought anything about it, for grown men in prison cried more than they wanted anyone to know.

He lifted his head and just sat there staring at the letter. It was finished now, finally finished. He held it in his hands while he worked to dry his tears. It was nearly two typewritten pages long. He knew it was longer than it needed to be, but there was so much he had to say. And so much he wanted to ask. And so much he needed to know.

He read his letter over several times, deciding against all changes. It said exactly what he had composed in his mind hours before. And that was enough. With trembling hands, he carefully folded the pages. Then he addressed the envelope with the address he had found on the scrap of paper. The letter was now inside. The envelope was now waiting to be sealed. It was all ready! It was on its way!

He mentally calculated the time it might take for his letter to arrive in El Paso and the time it would take for her to return to him. It would not take long. He just knew it would not.

Ordinarily, it would not take a letter long to go from Penjamo to El Paso and back. But what Rudolfo did not know was that Mexico was in the middle of an airline strike which severely affected anything or anyone using the airlines, including the postal service. His letter was being added to the stacks of hundreds of other letters being piled up in the mailbags in the back rooms of post offices in all the cities of Mexico. It was just as well that he did not know how long it would take his letter to reach the desk of Olivia S. D. de Lerin.

5

Postmark: Penjamo Jail

Olivia S. D. de Lerin was well known in El Paso, Texas. She served as the busy director of the department of Bible studies at the Baptist Spanish Publishing House. Some years before, she and her husband had taught in a number of schools in Mexico. She was constantly writing, copying, and editing Bible study notes and Sunday School lesson helps to be used by Spanish-speaking people on both sides of the US-Mexico border.

One of the first things she did each day was to turn her small desk calendar to the current date. Today was September 18. She then turned her attention to the correspondence for that day. She received a stack of mail daily from Latin America. Much of it required, or at least requested, an answer.

As she looked through the mail that day, something unusual caught her attention. A lot of the mail came from Mexico, so the postmark did not surprise her. She was somewhat startled by the return address: *Cárcel Municipal de Penjamo, Gto. Mex.—Penjamo City Jail, Guanajuato, Mexico.* Her first thought was that someone was playing a joke on her. As she began to read that neat typewritten letter, she knew it was for real.

In order to press on to the next writing assignment, she simply had to put the finished ones out of her mind. As editor of *El Expositor Biblico,* the adult Sunday School quarterly used by most of Latin America, she often wrote the brief devotional thought that appeared inside the front cover of each quarter's lesson book. It was a part of one such devotional based on the theme Be Thou Faithful that a desperate man had found crumpled in the courtyard of a jail in central Mexico.

She hardly recalled the particular editorial mentioned in the letter. She did have a file of all the editorials she had written. With the volume of writing she did, she certainly had to have some account of what she had used in which periodical. It took a while to locate that exact editorial. It had been written almost a full year before, so she pulled her file copy in order to better understand the situation which the Lord had so carefully placed in her hands. It read:

> In spite of the great advances of science, in spite of the fact that man has even walked on the moon, and has even been able to come back to earth to tell the inhabitants of what he has seen of that far-off satellite, the confusion worsens in the spiritual world, to the extent that sometimes we do not know in whom we humanly trust. . . . In this time there are some who say there's no reason to have an allegiance to anyone. . . . Every person can live the way he thinks best, without thought of anything or anyone.
>
> This is a time in which the home is being threatened even to destruction, and children have taken on the way of the world—they are living worldly lives, without taking into account any of the Christian morals. And then we read what it says in Revelation 2:8-10: "These things saith the first and the last, which was dead, and is alive; I know thy works, and tribulation, and poverty, (but thou art rich) and I know the blasphemy of them which say they are Jews, and are not, but are the synagogue of Satan. Fear none of those things which thou shalt suffer: behold, the devil shall cast some of you into prison, that ye may be tried; and ye shall have tribulation ten days: be thou faithful unto death, and I will give thee a crown of life."

The article continued onto the next page, but the scrap of it found by the prisoner had contained only this part. Rudolfo had somehow grasped the entire message, although only a part of it had been presented to him.

Olivia's eyes filled with tears. She placed the file copy of the article back in its place, then sat down at her desk with her hands folded in prayer across that letter. She felt as though she were in the very presence of God. Her lips moved in a silent prayer of thanksgiving to Him for what He had done for her that day. Her life goal as a writer had been affirmed. How often she had hoped that someone, somewhere, would be blessed by what she wrote. So many times she wondered if *anyone* was gaining anything from her writing. If she never knew it before, she certainly knew it now.

For what seemed like a long time, she just sat at her desk staring at the letter. She read it over and over and over. His request was so simple, yet so powerful. As many letters as she received in a year, she had never received one that said so sincerely, and yet so boldly, "If you're not ashamed to write a prisoner, please write me and tell me about your God."

As she put the letter on top of the stack of work she had planned to complete that day, she was unable to contain her emotions as she thought of this poor soul so thirsty to know of the Living Water of the Lord, having only one small scrap of paper containing only a few words about this living God. She couldn't help but wonder how this piece of a page of *El Expositor Biblico* had gotten to the jail in that little city. She did not know all about the missionary work in Mexico, but she was sure that there was no evangelical work of any denomination there in Penjamo.

After searching through some data that is always available to someone at a large publishing house like the Baptist Spanish Publishing House, she was even more sure that God directed that piece of paper to that prison, for she learned that not only was there no evangelical work of any denomination in Penjamo, there was none within 40 miles of that jail.

Olivia had waited long enough. With the same feeling she felt to open that letter before doing anything else that day, she could not contain the impulse to answer it now, immediately.

It was not her usual custom to answer any letter so quickly. She usually thought a while before writing a rough copy. After proofreading it, it was then ready to be typed. In the whole staff of the publishing house, there were dozens of employees, but only a few in the secretarial pool, so she had to type this letter herself. There was no time for a rough draft. She just let God guide her thoughts and fingers as she began her two-page reply. In part it said:

I want to answer your questions. In doing so, let me say that I *do* know God. I know Him as a loving Father Who receives as His child any that repents of his sins, no matter how black they may be. And the sinner man receives that forgiveness the moment he accepts Jesus Christ as his only and sufficient Saviour.

"God so loved the world, that he gave his only begotten Son, that whosoever believeth in Him should not perish, but have everlasting life." This Scripture [passage] comes from John 3:16 in the Holy Bible. I know this loving Father. Through His love for me and all mankind, He gave His only Son in order that He might pay the price for our sins by dying on Calvary's cross. This good and loving Father gave His Son in order that with His blood He could cleanse all my sins, your sins, and those of all who will repent. Because "the blood of Christ His Son cleanses us of all our sin." Only God is able to pardon our sins, and He does so freely.

She tried to answer all his questions in the simplest way she could. She assured him that no matter how bad he had been, God would pardon and forgive him if he would ask Him. She told him something about the way to do that. She told him how to use prayer. She encouraged him not to give up. She tried to help him overcome his doubt, as expressed in his letter, that even though he did not know God, God knew him.

In the simplest words possible, she assured him that God was concerned about him, and that she loved him too—as a creation of God—and was not in the least bit ashamed to write to him. She included some Bible study materials and directed him to several marked passages in the Gospel of John which she enclosed with the letter.

With hands trembling with excitement, she addressed a large manila envelope. With a prayer, she placed the letter, the study materials, and the Gospel of John inside. It had taken five and one-half weeks for his letter to make the roundabout trip to El Paso. She hoped her reply would not take nearly that long to get back to Penjamo. Even though she did not know Rudolfo Halcon personally, she knew enough about that burning desire in his heart to know that a desperate man was anxiously and patiently awaiting the reply in a lonely cell in the municipal jail of Penjamo, Mexico.

6
Your Sins Will Find You Out

Rudolfo *was* desperate and he *was* anxiously waiting for Olivia S. D. de Lerin's reply; but he was *not* waiting too patiently. It had been weeks since that rainy afternoon when he found the scrap of paper. He knew when he sent the letter that it would probably take a few weeks for it to arrive in El Paso. He even anticipated that it would take a little time for her answer to come back to him. Because of that, he did not even begin to look for a reply for the first couple of weeks.

During those weeks, his day-to-day routine remained the same. The only thing that changed was the hope that dwelt within him now. He had not dared mention that scrap of paper to anyone else. If for some reason all this with the letter did not work out, he felt it was better to keep it to himself. That way he would not feel so bad.

Every afternoon he repeated his prison job. Sweeping the courtyard gave him reason to recall all that happened. Finding that piece of paper had made him more aware of the trash that was there. Even though he never found anything else of much interest, it took him longer to finish the task because he began to read almost everything he picked up. For two weeks he did this to help pass the time.

By the time the third week arrived, his anticipation was at a peak. When the third week came and went without a word, he just knew with every mail call that it would arrive. His anticipation slowly diminished, gradually reverting to those old feelings of frustration and disappointment.

Days passed by him again. Before finding that scrap of paper, his life had been a meaningless routine. Back then he did not expect much. He also never got much; but that was OK, for he had very little hope for each new day. How he had hoped that now there would be a difference. How stupid he had been! How foolish he felt now when he thought of putting his hope in a little piece of scrap paper.

It had always seemed like a good thing to have hope in something. From an early age he had been taught to build one's hope on the future. In later years he had learned that one could certainly have hope that there would be gain through personal investments. And one always felt more secure with a comfortable little bank account. A man could hope for a promotion in his job or blessings in his family; but for a man as mature and smart as he thought himself to be, to hang his hope onto a torn piece of paper was almost senseless, ridiculous. Why didn't he realize that before?

For all he knew, that paper scrap had come from some article written years before. That would not change the truth—if any—contained there. But for all he knew, the publishing house that printed it was not even in business anymore. And even if it was, the woman who wrote the article might not answer him. For all he knew, she did not even work there now; and the people at the publishing house might not know where to forward his letter. And even if they did not know where to send it, to do so would only take more time. And he did not feel he had the time to wait.

He felt so defeated again. When a man is low, it doesn't take much more to beat him down even lower. When a man is weak, he does not fight back in the same way as before. Even though this battle was taking place only in his own mind, he did not have the resources at hand to do much about it. He continued to think negative thoughts. Maybe he really was doomed to spend the rest of his days confined to these few walls and rooms, without hope. After all, he had done a mean thing to some very trusting people. What he had done was called fraud. And he had gotten caught at it. Otherwise, he'd not even be in jail at all.

It is hard to say exactly when it all started. For most of his adult years, he had wanted to make something of himself. Hardly anyone else in his family had become a professional in any area. He studied hard and got into law school. His first years there had been good ones. He was really dedicated to learning and being the best student he could be. Even though it was a sacrifice for him to be away from home so much, he felt it was worth it for the future of his family.

A good lawyer made good money, but for him his drive was about something much more than good money. He was conscious of the many, many ways he could be of some help to the people of his own country who often needed a good lawyer. At the beginning, he had high ideals and goals, and these motivated him to try to become all that he could in order to help others and to serve mankind.

He was over halfway through law school when he heard some fellow students talking about doing some law practice even before they finished their degree program. They were convinced that they knew just enough to go ahead and start practicing their profession. He heard them talk about the money they could make even then.

He began thinking, Hey, I'm as smart as they are. And I'm educated and intelligent. So he talked to them and learned what they planned to do. Their plan, although a bit crooked, did not sound too bad even to a person like him with such high ideals.

They were going to pass themselves off as full-fledged lawyers. Unsuspecting clients would pay them a healthy down payment for services which they would pretend to be doing. After a while they would simply say that it was legally impossible to follow through. There were all kinds of legal terms one could use to convince a person of that. People also knew that at times the wheels of justice turned much slower than they wished. It would not be hard—just keep the down payment, or at least part of it, then go on to another city with other people, other cases, other healthy down payments. Repeat the same legal scam all over again. Make a lot of money for doing a little work. It sounded good.

Why not? he thought. What do I have to lose?

One thing he did not think about losing was his self-respect; for another, the good opportunities that lay ahead. If only he had finished his studies, he could have become the helpful lawyer he set out to be. When he asked himself that question, What do I have to lose?, he probably never thought that this fraudulent scheme might cause him to lose his family. He also had not given a lot of thought to the possibility that he might lose something else quite important to him—his life!

He began doing all the things he and the other students had talked about. For a while it was going quite well. He could not believe how trusting people were. They seldom asked to see his credentials and hardly ever wanted to know about his practice and experience and background. There were times when his conscience grieved him a little, like the time that elderly couple had handed over almost all their life savings in order to pay for his legal services, or when someone sold part of his property to pay for Rudolfo's "fees." It was at those times he wished he had never started doing things like this. It was a little late to back down now, for he was caught up in his own scam and did not really want to stop.

For years he got by with it. Then one day he was finally caught, arrested on the spot, and taken to the nearest jail—Penjamo. There was no judge. There was no trial. There was no opportunity to make a phone call to his family. There was no offer to call his lawyer, even if he had had one. The only lawyers he knew were faculty members at school, and he knew what kind of help he would get from them.

He might have called his fellow "lawyers," although at times like this, he was sure his student friends would forget about their loyalties. He had no clothes other than the suit he was wearing at the time. He did have one thing, however. He had a genuinely good ability for taking advantage of others. He also had a healthy reputation for defrauding people. So off he went to jail!

It took a while, but little by little the authorities learned most of the details about his life-style. Most of his clients had come to him based on reputation or word of mouth; so when the news about his arrest began to spread, many of the people he had tricked came forward to tell their side of the story. It wasn't a very pretty story. They had a strong case against him. He had taken quite a lot of money from many innocent and trusting people.

Someone in a higher position might have gotten away with it, but not a middle-aged law student. It was then that they found out about his house and made the necessary arrangements to go there, evict his family, and take his house and personal possessions. They would be sold, and the money would be used to help pay back some of what he had taken from those innocent people. It would also help to pay off the debts he had compiled during his years of dishonesty, cheating, and fraud.

It had all sounded so simple and innocent when he and his fellow students began talking about it that day many years ago. What had gone wrong? He could not help but recall a phrase that he had heard all his life: *To be sure, your sins will find you out.* That phrase had come true in his life. Although he had been brought up to know right from wrong, he had strayed from those good teachings. When did he change? What had happened to all those good things he wanted to do and be? He had had hopes and dreams, but they turned out completely different than he had ever imagined.

His plan to write a woman in El Paso and the hope he held for some answer from her had turned out somewhat different too. But that was just another thing that had gone wrong, and he did not know why.

7
Like Sheep Without a Shepherd

It was about that same time that Socorro made a promise to the Virgin Saint—if her husband were released, she would make a pilgrimage in the Virgin's honor. To people who live in parts of the world where there are not such things as promises made to the Virgin Saint or pilgrimages made in her honor, perhaps a bit of explanation is due here.

In the place where Socorro grew up, there was a strong belief in the image of a woman—believed to be the Virgin Mary—who had wondrously and miraculously appeared to a shepherd boy one day. From that time until the present, people accepted this appearance as a miracle, and many of the people of Socorro's country truly believed that she would hear and honor their requests.

At difficult times, when all else seemed so distant, they made dedicated and reverent vows to her that if she would help them, they would honor her in some special way. The most common way was to make a pilgrimage to the city where her image was kept. These trips were often made in large groups in order that they could support each other during the trip, as well as share the companionship. Once the pilgrims arrived at the elaborate cathedral built especially to house the Virgin's image, the common practice was to walk the entire length of the long stone aisle on their knees. They felt this showed the Virgin even more of their genuine desire for repentance and thanksgiving.

Socorro was ready to do all this and more. As she said, she'd try anything now!

During her pilgrimage, she had a lot of time to think. As she wearily walked the miles leading up to the basilica, she could not help but remember those days after they had been thrown out of their house. Even though it sometimes made her sad to relive those unpleasant days, the memories also gave her courage to go on.

As she walked, she thought. Two pans, an armful of clothes, a handful of books—those were the few things she had salvaged that awful day. They had been five lonely people feeling like lost sheep. The pans would come in handy when they had more food. The stack of tortillas which they left home with had disappeared that very first night. After all, those five lost sheep were also hungry!

Of all the things they needed at the moment, the handful of books was not on the list. She really had not thought of that the day she swept them off the floor. She had no idea what the books even were. She did not know one of the books just happened to be a small Gideon New Testament.

After some time, she learned the details of her husband's arrest. She visited him in jail. He was so ashamed he could hardly talk to her. And even when he spoke, his eyes turned away from her as he tried to tell her how he felt.

"Oh, I'm so ashamed of what I've done. Not only because of what I've done to myself, but I'm ashamed of what I've done to you. Socorro, I'm suffering for myself. But I'm suffering even more because of what is happening to you and the children. I promise you that ..."

"No, Rudolfo," Socorro interrupted him. "Don't make any promises right now. Wait a while. There is no reason for you to promise us anything." She was a wise wife who knew that promises made when one could not keep them made a person feel even worse.

"But let me promise you something, my husband. Your

wife and children will always be here for you. Even though things have sort of fallen apart for us right now, we have all the time in the future to put it all back together again."

"Oh, Socorro, I'm not worthy of all your love and attention."

"When I married you, I married you for the good times and for the bad. It has nothing whatever to do with whether a person is worthy of love and attention."

"But there are so many things I need to say."

"There will be time for all that. Right now there isn't anything else that needs to be said."

"Thank you for coming today. And thank you for assuring me of all those things. I was so afraid you would leave me now."

"We will never desert you, Rudolfo. You have our word for that."

That was an easy thing to say. It had been more difficult to carry out; for at the moment she said it, she and the children had no plans or any place to go. Her sister had said they could live with her if they would have nothing more to do with Rudolfo, who was now thought of not as a good relative but as a bad criminal. Socorro just could not make that choice. She knew he had done many wrong things in his life, but she could not turn her back on him now. So she and her little flock—sheep without a shepherd—decided to just stay there in Penjamo.

For several days the children spent much of their time playing in the plaza while Socorro looked for work. They watched as other children ran up to everyone who walked through the plaza begging for a few coins or something to eat. They saw how those wealthier people eating at the sidewalk restaurants and corner taco stands gave the hungry children scraps of meat and bread. It was very difficult for them to believe that they had come to this. It was all but impossible for them to hold out their hands to beg. But when the stomach begins to hurt so badly for lack of food, it becomes easier to do things one has never done before.

It was even harder for the wife of a formerly successful businessman to believe they had come to this place in life. She just could not bring herself to beg. It was wrong! She had been raised in an environment where one never begged for anything. Their circumstances were made even harder by the fact that Socorro had never held a job a day in her life. She had no trade. She had no skill. For years, though, she had been a good wife and mother, so she knew she could cook and clean a house. Although she did not want to leave the children at this time, she knew what she had to do. She began walking through the city knocking on doors, hoping to find someone who needed just her kind of a cook and housekeeper.

It did not take her long to find someone who would give her a try sight unseen. It was hard at first being someone's servant and cook and cleaning woman. But each time she began to feel sorry for herself she thought about her husband. He sat there in the corner of a dirty jail cell alone and forlorn. She could not do anything about that right now. There was a more pressing need. She had to find a place for her and the children to live. They could not just sleep on the sidewalk, although many others did so.

For days they slept wherever they could. And that was hard. She had hoped to be paid a little money at the beginning of her work, but had to wait until after the first full week. But with her first money she was finally able to afford a little corner room in an old condemned building. In other years it had likely been a really fine place, as evidenced by the typically Mexican courtyard in the center. Now the grass and bushes had grown completely out of control and had all but overrun the place. Most of the windows were broken out and the walls and ceilings were all but falling, but this is where they lived for a while. At least they were all alive and they still had each other.

As Socorro walked toward the basilica, all those thoughts made her even more sure that she was doing the only right thing. As the pilgrimage group arrived at the basilica, she got into position on her knees at the opposite end of the plaza. She had much to be thankful for. She wanted to express her spirit of gratitude by crawling across the stone plaza and down the long tiled aisle of the church on her knees.

By doing even more penance, she was sure that even the people walking through the plaza that day could see and know of her attitude of thanksgiving. They would know that she was truly serving the one who had so miraculously kept them alive and given them a life together and a place to live. When her husband was released from jail, she prayed that they would all be able to return and give thanks again. At the moment she simply wanted to keep crawling toward the door, recalling the reason why she had taken this pilgrimage—her gratitude.

She was grateful that the oldest son, Rudolfo, Jr., was the first of the children to go to work. With the few extra pesos she had been able to spare him, he set up a little shoeshine stand in the plaza. He did not have one of those fancy chairs with iron supports on which well-dressed men could rest their fine shoes. His was a simple wooden box with a sloping top. At the very beginning he realized that when a man walked away with a good shoeshine, that was a lot more important to him than the kind of box on which he had rested his foot.

Another thing young Rudolfo learned was the art of conversation. He did not exactly play on the emotions of his wealthier clients; but while he held them by the foot, he often touched their hearts as well with a story about his father, who was in jail just on the other side the plaza, and how he was trying to help support his family in the meantime. Many of the men were touched by his story and paid him more than the going price for a shoeshine. Others merely listened with interest as he reached underneath the footrest into that little tray which held his two cans of polish. The cans, one black and the other brown, were about all the equipment he had or needed, except for his small brush and a polish rag or two.

It was hard work for a boy who had never had to do any kind of odd job before. Furthermore, it was a humiliating experience to kneel on the concrete there in the plaza and shine shoes. But at least it was a steady and honest work which brought in a few more centavos for the family. For that, Socorro was most grateful. Combined with what her simple job paid, she was able to take care of her little flock in a better way. Since the children had been taken out of school when they left to come here, the younger ones spent most of their days in and around the vacant lot that surrounded "their house."

The pilgrimage had been over for some time now. She was back at Penjamo, where life had resumed its sameness. She tried repeating her vow, but after a while it was evident that it was not accomplishing the good she hoped it would. When after a while it had not gained Rudolfo's immediate release, she knew she had to do something else. She remembered that little New Testament she had picked up that day. She decided to go back and read it. Like so many people, she had tried everything else first!

8
That Gideon New Testament

That Gideon New Testament had come to her in a most unusual way, a mysterious way. She had gone out to the open market early one morning to buy fresh fruits and vegetables. There were some people who preferred buying their produce from the large grocery store just a block off the main square, but she had formed a longtime habit of going to the street market. She had grown to trust the farmers who arrived in the predawn darkness with their trucks full to running over with yesterday's garden goods. She knew that as fresh as they were in the morning, that the later hours in the day would show that the heat and air had wilted the greens and made the peas and beans swell.

After the children got off to school, she usually headed for the open market. Buying fresh foods and cooking for her family gave Socorro a good feeling in her heart. Marketing was also something of a social outing in a life that often lacked other more normal opportunities to mix and mingle with the people. It was something of "her time" to be able to visit with the other housewives in her neighborhood. Although she seldom visited in their homes or had them visit in hers, she knew a lot about them as families. While waiting for the vegetable man to weigh the potatoes or tomatoes, there was always a minute to ask about the health of the children, how the father of the family was doing in finding a job, or about the other pressures of the world in which they found themselves struggling to make ends meet day after day.

The day she received the New Testament she did not feel especially spiritual. She had absolutely no thought of God or of reading the Holy Scriptures as she went about her rather routine task of sampling the grapes, weighing the tomatoes, or smelling the onions. She was minding her own business, walking along in the middle of the bustling crowd, when a little old man came up to her. He looked her right in the eye and thrust a small book into her hands. He did not say anything or offer to make any explanation. He just gave her the book, a New Testament, and quickly disappeared into the crowded market.

Socorro had two choices at that moment. She could either accept the book or let it drop from her hand there in the marketplace. She held on to it, although she wondered about the significance of it. She had never seen a book like it, but a quick glance at its contents quickly convinced her that there was no harm in keeping it. She took it home, and without so much as a second thought added it to the stack of other books already in the bookcase.

In all of this time she had never opened it again. She was quite sure that no one else had either. It had remained there until that day when they were thrown out. Now, as she began to read, she had no doubt as to why it had been thrust into her life.

She knew absolutely nothing about the Bible, but she had to read no further than the first words inside the front cover to find some encouragement. The first words printed at the top of the page were *Auxilio en tiempo de necesidad* (Help in time of need).

Her eyes quickly scanned the list of "helps." There were helps for finding peace and others for helping build up one's courage. There were verses to read when one needed special help in order to find relief, guidance, and rest. Other scriptural helps were there for that time when a person was without comfort or needed added strength. According to this list, there were passages to read that would help a person encounter salvation.

Salvation from what? she wondered aloud. To find out, it was suggested that she read John 3:3. It was confusing to her at first. She did not understand such phrases as *born again* and *the kingdom of God.* Romans 10:9 spoke of confession. She was familiar with confession, but not with what it said about believing in her heart and being saved. She finally found a verse she had heard before in John 3:16. Even though she did not understand it at all, she read on.

The helps listed many Scripture verses one could read for praise and rejoicing. She did not feel much like doing that right now, but she looked up one or two of them just to see what they said. Finding passages from Hebrews and James or others would have been nearly impossible for her had there not been page numbers beside the suggested verses. Someone had known that people like her would be using this book. And they had planned it in such a way as to make it possible for her to find exactly what she needed to read at the moment. In 1 Thessalonians 5:18 she read that it was the will of God that she give thanks in everything. How could she possibly give thanks for everything that was going wrong in her life at this time? And how could this possibly be the will of God for her?

She did not really know how to pray, but she mouthed a simple one before reading on. She seemed to feel better just trying to do what the Scriptures told her to do. How she wished she could truly identify with that person who wrote those words she found in 2 Corinthians 12:8-10 about taking pleasure in persecutions and distresses. She did feel weak, but that did not make her feel strong in the Lord.

How she wanted to feel that the Lord's grace was enough. How she wished that His strength could be made perfect in her weakness. Again she said some words asking the God of heaven to help her accept her trials. And almost immediately she again felt something happening in her life.

These words of God seemed to be written there especially for her. She could hardly wait to read the next one. "For peace in time of anxiety, read Philippians 4:6-7, page 362." She quickly found the passage and read it. It did not seem possible. That was all too easy. It was impossible to think about living without worrying about anything. But it said to pray and tell God your requests. He would then give a peace in your time of anxiety that you would not be able to understand. Not only would He give one that peace, but He would keep that person peaceful through Jesus.

Why hadn't she ever opened this wonderful book before? It seemed to have the answer for every need she had ever had. The promises of God spoke directly to her in every verse. The assurances that Jesus gave His confused disciples were exactly what she needed for the confusion in her own life. The hope that was expressed in this wonderful little book was about all the hope she had at the moment. But how could she ever tell Rudolfo? After all, for years he had had no interest in religion or the Bible. Maybe she'd just keep it all to herself. Or maybe in God's good time He would give her the opportunity she needed to tell her husband and family. For now, she just kept reading. And believing.

The more she read, the more she believed. And the more she believed, the more she knew why God had allowed her to keep that book when almost everything else had been taken away from her.

9
No One Cares About Me

Socorro was worried about how she was going to tell her husband about the peace and love and encouragement and hope she found while reading the New Testament. Rudolfo had his own worries. He had never really thought much about the passing of time before, but now he was preoccupied with it.

It had been a full two years since his awful arrest—two years of sitting in a jail cell, two years since his family had been thrown out into the street. It had been only a few weeks since he found that crumpled piece of paper in the courtyard. But in ways those few weeks since he wrote to Olivia S. D. de Lerin had seemed longer than all the other weeks combined. Waiting was something at which he was not particularly effective. Patience was a virtue he needed to develop. Even as a young boy, he was always busy, always going, always doing something.

He had grown up in a rather simple family. For the most part, they did what their grandfathers had done before them. Their life-style was one of rural people who enjoyed simple pleasures. They spent a lot of time doing things together. They were not what one would call craftsmen; but they did design, make, and sell typical Mexican crafts. People knew about baskets and purses and they could always count on his family being of a higher quality than others'.

His family was also a typical one; so was his boyhood. His

father was the dominant figure that most Mexican men think themselves to be. His mother also fit the rather typical Mexican housewife who enjoyed the simple things. She always had a yard full of flowers and she could make the best smelling soup out of almost anything. She was the one who got the children ready for early Mass and she was the parent who went with them.

Church had never been too important for Rudolfo, although later in his boyhood years he was chosen to serve as an altar boy in his local church. He attended mostly because his mother wanted him to. He went through all the training and the learning processes; but by his teenage years he saw so much of what he felt was false in the church and its leadership that he became disillusioned not only about the benefit of working in the church but of putting too much faith in a religious system that seemed to focus more on the human side of it all excluding God. That did not really matter much to him for he did not put much faith in God.

He married young. He had many hopes and dreams for his rapidly growing family. He had aspirations for a professional law career. His family encouraged him to study, so he did. All those plans went along well until he began to focus on money and self instead of the genuine service he could perform for others. He would give almost anything to go back a few years, giving himself another chance to make it without going to such extremes. He knew it was a ridiculous thought. All he could do now was wait.

He could hardly believe that men like him, locked away behind steel gates day and night, had nothing to do but wait. He had not used his hands to make anything for a long time now, but he recalled how his family had made and marketed things when he was a boy. Maybe the prisoners could do something like that. It could be a form of learning as well as some good training for the future. It could not be too hard to get something started, although it would not be exactly like the way his family used to do it.

He and his brothers had used the best reeds and straw and stones and sticks they could afford in order to make the plaques and baskets and *adornos* they sold in the marketplace. Every week they went to the Sunday market in the nearby town to sell their wares. As a youngster he always looked forward to that. It was about the only time they got out of town.

Early on Sunday morning, they would gather up the baskets and bags of handmade goods and walk to that place at the end of the dusty road that led to their house and wait for the large bus to take them to market. As much as he liked the bus ride, he liked it even better when the bus would be late or full and somebody would come along in a pickup truck and give them a ride into town. There was something especially exciting about standing up and facing the wind and watching the world blow by all around you.

How he wished he could feel that fresh air on his face right then. The air in his cell seemed to be taking lessons from the time—both were standing still. He reached under his pillow and found that crumpled piece of paper, now pressed smooth by time and numerous readings, and began to read. Reading it had become a nightly routine. He read it over and over and over. "Be thou faithful unto death, and I will give thee a crown of life. Be thou faithful unto death, and I will give thee a crown of life. Be thou faithful unto death, and I will give thee a crown of life."

I'm trying, he thought. But it doesn't seem to be making a lot of sense. After all, I've been locked in here for two years already and I've never even been brought to trial. They keep saying they'll finally get around to it. What's the use of it all? I wrote that woman in El Paso almost a month ago. She's not going to help me. She probably doesn't even care. No one can help me understand all that's happening to me. Maybe it would really be better to just end it all. I think everyone would be better off without me.

He read the verse again. "Faithful . . . unto . . . death . . . God . . . crown of life." Ha! No one cares about me. Not even God! With that, he crumpled the worn paper into a tight little ball and was on the verge of throwing it out the open door back into the patio where he'd found it when he had a second thought; and after smoothing it out the best he could, he stuck it back under his pillow. After all, it seemed to be the only hope he had—and even that seemed to be fading.

It was 4:00 A.M., September 25. It had been a month and a half since he wrote to El Paso. He couldn't sleep. For days he had been unable to sleep. He was almost afraid to go to sleep. In his nightmares he seemed to always be so close to death. Even in his wakening moments he had been thinking about ending his life again. He tossed, turned, and paced. For hours now he had been desperately trying to find some answers for it all. Even though he had the liberty to walk around in the room which served as his cell and he was totally free to roam around in the courtyard outside, his spirit felt bound as if by heavy chains. The night was quiet and calm and peaceful, but inside his own heart he could find no peace and quiet.

He found himself thinking of that spiritual confusion which the article had talked about. He wanted to read it just one more time, yet he dared not turn on the light. He did not need the light. He did not have to read the message on the paper anymore. He had it all memorized—every word of every line. He found it under his pillow where he had kept it all these weeks. It had become everything to him. Just thinking about it seemed to calm him down now. And just think, there had been a brief moment when he had almost thrown it away. What would he have done without it had he followed that impulse? How glad he was that he hadn't. He did not sleep anymore that night, but spent the rest of the night lying on his cot thinking.

He hardly noticed when the sun came up that day. There was nothing to look forward to anymore; so he just lay there, his body tossing, his mind wandering aimlessly in thought. He was jolted by the voice of the guard at the front gate. The guard was shouting his name at top volume.

"Halcon. Halcon. Halcon, you got a visitor at the front gate."

A visitor? he thought. Who would be visiting me? Especially at this time of day? Maybe it's my lawyer. Maybe I'm finally coming to trial.

He sprang out of bed anticipating something good. His room was the first one inside the gate; he could see immediately who was there. It was not his lawyer. It was his wife standing just on the other side of the heavy steel gate.

What's she doing here? he thought. This isn't even visiting day. He pulled on his pants and put on his wrinkled white shirt and went out to see what this was all about.

Her first words were that same question she'd asked for weeks now. "Have you received an answer to your letter?"

"Forget about that letter!" he almost shouted back. "Nobody cares about me. No one wants to hear about me. No one wants to help me. I've given up hope of ever hearing from her, so let's forget about that letter."

"Oh, no, my husband. We can't do that. Just last night I had a dream. In my dream I asked you that question—Have you received an answer to your letter?—and just as you did a moment ago, you told me you'd lost hope and to forget about the letter. But in my dream a letter came, a beautiful letter, a letter with a lot of the answers you are waiting to hear. When I came today, I felt sure you had received it. That's why I asked. But wait, my husband. Wait just a little longer. I know it will come. I just know it. I must go now or I'll be late for work."

From the front gate of the prison one could look directly out into the street through the open wooden doors of the front office. So he watched Socorro as she crossed the street and disappeared into the already busy plaza. He stood there a long time thinking about what she'd said. It just didn't make sense. Dreams? Everyone knows that dreams never come true.

He tried not to think too much about what she said. He tried to keep himself busy for a while after she left. He cleaned up his room, washed his face. He even decided to shave that day, although it was against his usual practice of waiting until night. As he stood at the sink, he caught himself staring at the face he saw in the mirror. How he wished he could figure all this out. He drifted off into daydreams of other times in other places until the splash of cold water brought him back to the reality of the day. He was still lost in thought when he heard his name being called out by the guard at the front gate.

"Halcon. Halcon. Rudolfo Halcon, there's a package here for you."

He didn't even take the time to put his basin and towel back in his room. He ran to the gate. The guard was holding it out through the bars in the gate—a big brown manila envelope. As he got to the gate, the guard was reading the address.

"Señor Rudolfo Halcon, City Jail, Penjamo, Guanajuato, Mexico. And it's from a Señora Lerin, Baptist Spanish Publishing House, El Paso, Texas. You're lucky to get this, Rudolfo. We're lucky to get any mail these days with the airline strike and all. My wife's brother lives in Laredo, and he wrote us about two months ago that it was taking mail more than twice the usual time to get anyplace in the country. And mail crossing the border was really taking its time. Why, he said that one of the letters we wrote him didn't even leave Mexico until three weeks after it was dated. And his letter back to us took . . ."

The guard continued talking as he handed him the package. Rudolfo did not hear him anymore, however. He was standing there at the front gate to the city jail of Penjamo holding a big brown manila envelope, thinking all the time that Socorro was right. All of this *was* a dream all right. But a dream come true!

10

Peace, Pardon, and Joy

It was something of a miracle that he held that package in his hands at all. He had sent his letter on August 11. It was now September 25. But the guard had said something about an airline strike in Mexico. An airline strike? No wonder it had taken so long! If only he had known. All those negative, doubting thoughts were forgotten, for in his hands he held something for which he had waited a long time.

As he walked back to that little *rincon* of a cell, carefully and lovingly clutching the envelope, the strangest sort of feeling came over him. He could not have explained it, even if anyone had asked him about it. It was a different kind of feeling. It was something mysterious. It was something wonderful! It was more than just the hair standing up on the back of his neck. It was peaceful, but at the same time exciting.

If he'd had to put this feeling into words, he would not have been capable of doing so. It was something of the same kind of feeling he had felt when he found that scrap of paper in the patio almost two months before. He could relate this feeling to the one he got when he first read the words written on that paper. He related it to a feeling he had tried to imagine once when he thought how it might be in the very presence of God.

He only knew that he felt like a little boy again, a little boy

47

about to open a gift—knowing, yet not really knowing, what was inside the package. He slowly and deliberately opened the clasp on the envelope and slid his finger inside the flap. He carefully took out the contents, holding each piece of paper, each page, and each book as he looked at them individually, as though he had uncovered something highly sacred. To him they almost were. There were the letter and the books and the home Bible studies, just as she had sent them. He wanted to look at everything at once, but first he decided to read her letter.

He read it so fast the first time that he missed some of what she told him. He read it the second time slowly and carefully. She had answered all of his questions. She told him in words he could understand about her personal belief in a loving and forgiving God Who loved him too. He could hardly believe that God loved him so much that He would send His Son Jesus to die for him.

As he read on, he felt the chains of Satan that had bound his spirit so tightly in sin begin to slacken and slip away. As he read, he felt the pardon that was his for the asking. So many times he had thought about being pardoned, forgiven, and freed.

Here she wrote: "Only God is able to pardon our sins, and He does so freely. The Apostle John says, 'My little children, these things write I unto you, that ye sin not. And if any man sin, we have an advocate with the Father, Jesus Christ the righteous.' Thus, surely, you can understand that God will have mercy on you and give to you that which you desire—peace, pardon, and joy."

Peace? Pardon? Joy? For me? he questioned. And it's all free? The warm and loving arms of God suddenly seemed very real to him. It was not just something he was reading about, it was something he was experiencing. Tears came to his eyes as he began to read the marked verses in the Bible she had enclosed.

He had never had his own copy of the sacred Scriptures. He seemed to recall in the back of his mind seeing a Testament at one time or another, possibly in his own house, but he'd never read it. The rituals and traditions of his boyhood church did not encourage the people to have their own copy. Even in recent years, his wife and children had been discouraged by that same church from having a personal Bible. The church's idea was that the church leaders would be able to explain the Bible to anyone who needed to know, and there was no need for people to read and study it for themselves. Now he held a portion of it in his very own hands. It was only a small copy of the Gospel of John, but it was the first time that it had seemed so important.

The first verse she'd marked for him to read was John 3:16, the one she'd used in her letter that told him about God's love and everlasting life. Every time he thought of that, he found it hard to believe that God loved him and *wanted* him to have an everlasting life. Next she had instructed him to read John 10:7-10. In those verses Jesus Himself was talking about sheep and thieves and the abundant life He came to give. In John 8:34-35 he read about being a slave to sin. He read about truth and freedom through belief in Jesus. There it was again. Talk about freedom! He was beginning to understand now. Sin separates a person from God and deprives him of the life eternal. So one can only be free as he searches for and finds the True One.

It was like unraveling the tangled strings of his life. His hands could hardly turn to the next Scripture verse fast enough. John 1:29 told him how he could have his sins taken away by the Lamb of God. It was just as Olivia S. D. de Lerin had said. Jesus not only came to take away her sins but also his and the sins of the entire world. God's Perfect Son came to die on the cross in order that He could take away his sins.

Rudolfo could scarcely contain his tears. He was not just reading a letter, he was listening to the personal voice of God. Never in his life had he felt this way before. Of course, never in his life had he known the truth before. He had no idea of the way to truth and life through Jesus Christ. How often he had tried to do it all on his own. He had struggled so much to find some peace. How he had hoped for pardon. He had lived all of his life without knowing that genuine joy. It was all available to him now. And there was no other way but through Jesus Christ, the Saviour. He could become a son of God. All he had to do was to believe.

When he first began looking for the verses, he was confused by the chapter and the verse numbers. Now after only a few minutes of searching the Scriptures, he felt much more secure. He turned immediately to the next verses she had suggested. He was like a starving man, hungering now to feed on the Bread of life so personally described in John 6:35. Suddenly he thought not only of himself but of his wife and children. They too were hungry and thirsty both physically and spiritually. Jesus was the only One Who could satisfy the spiritual hunger and thirst. He could hardly wait for Thursday to come so he could share all this with them. He wanted to tell them about all that God had told him through reading this Gospel of John.

At the end of the Scripture verses was a prayer. He'd never prayed a sincere prayer in his life before now. Oh, he had repeated words before, but not like now. He read it through. It seemed so simple. So he prayed it aloud. For the first time in his life, he said:

> I know that Christ died for me on the cross, and that He now lives eternally. At this very moment, I want Him to listen to my prayer. I confess that I'm a sinner, and I don't deserve anything but the judgment of God for my sins. But I now ask Christ to pardon me and to change my life. I accept Him as the personal Lord and Saviour of my life.

The miracle was now complete. What had begun as the simple act of cleaning up a jail courtyard had led to the discovery of that piece of paper. But even before that, God had taken away all that Rudolfo thought he had to have in order to have an abundant life and had allowed him to be in this place. Now a package had come, bringing with it the words of a friend and the salvation that comes only through the Lord Jesus Christ. His prayer was over, but his new life had just begun.

11
The Family of God

It didn't take God long to give Rudolfo some special opportunities to share his newfound faith. One of those special times was the one he had looked forward to with his own family. Thursdays were visiting days at the jail. And during the very next visit, he told Socorro and his sons and daughters all about God and His love for folks like them.

They had barely gotten into the visiting area when he burst out with, "I really don't know how you're going to take this, but there's something very important I've got to tell you. You aren't the only visitors I've had this week."

Socorro interrupted him long enough to ask, "Who, Rudolfo? Who has been here and filled you with so much excitement?"

He continued without a pause. "A few days ago I had the opportunity to receive a very special visitor here." This time the children were the ones whose curiosity made them yell out in the singsongy way, "Papa's had a visitor. A very important visitor. Who was it, Papa? Tell us. Who?"

Holding his hands out to them, indicating that they should settle down and listen, he leaned toward them as he said, "His name was Jesus."

Almost in unison, Socorro and the children said, "Jesus?"

"Yes, Jesus. I know you probably don't understand. Let me try to explain. I'm so sorry I never let Him into my life before. If I had, I might not have been in this trouble, and you might not have to be living like you are. But right now I'm glad to have been here. This is where God wanted me to be. This is where He put me so I would listen to Him. You see, Jesus lived a long time ago. His Father, God, sent Him to earth as a living sacrifice for all the people. He loved us so much that there was nothing else He could have done. And for those who really believe in Him, there is a wonderful life awaiting them in heaven. You see, this Jesus died here. He was crucified on a cross, but He didn't stay dead. He rose to live again in the hearts of those who would believe on Him.

"One of the things I hope you can do is decide to accept Him too as your personal Lord and Saviour. I don't want you to do it just because I did. I want you to do so because you know it's the right thing to do and because you know you can't continue to do everything on your own. Believe me, God wants to help you too, just as He has helped me. He wants to save you from your sin and help you live as His children."

Socorro burst into tears. She could not help but think about what she had been reading in her own New Testament. She didn't even have to worry about how she was going to tell her husband what she was thinking. God had already told him in another special way. The children all gathered around him, although they did not completely understand all that their father was saying.

They did realize, however, that something very important had happened to him, and this thing that had happened was something significant and life-changing. He was different today. If this wonderful and important thing had made such a difference in him, they all knew it was something good. It was something that they needed to happen to them too. But no one said anything at that moment. No one knew exactly what to say. As he said, it would come to them when they were ready for it, when they realized their need for it, and when they asked for it.

The spiritual changes that happened to the family didn't happen all at once, but one by one they too accepted the Lord as their personal Saviour just as he had done. They all assured Rudolfo that they did not make their decisions just because he had made his personal decision. In their own particular way, each one of them had a genuine and personally convicting experience with God. And all of this happened without a church. All of it happened without a preacher. All of it happened without a missionary. A small family of people who had lost their home, their car, their possessions, had now found that "kingdom and God and His righteousness," and they knew now that "all the other things would be added" as God thought best.

Family visiting days after that became worship days, for they spent some time during each visit reading the Bible together and praying with one another. They had always been a close family. Now they were even closer—as part of the family of God. With his family praying for him, constantly asking God that he would be used in a special way, he asked God to let him become a strong witness for Him right there in the jail. It did not take long for God to take him at his word.

On one of those nights when he lay awake—praying now, not worrying about tomorrow—he went outside just so he could look up and see the stars. Except for that one night not long ago which he spent on the steps outside his cell, he'd not taken time to look at the night sky. Now it represented something of the closeness of his God. There was another light in the courtyard that caught his attention. A very dim light shown from the shower house across the patio. It made him a little suspicious. He recalled how he had tried to sneak out there some weeks ago.

Everyone else seemed to be asleep. The few steps that took him to the half-enclosed toilet on the other side of the yard brought him face-to-face with another prisoner. Rudolfo recognized him as a man who'd only come just a day or two before. He was a quiet type who had hardly spoken a word to any of the other men in those couple of days. He did his work, but had a hard time adjusting to things. That was not too unusual. It always took a man a few days to accept the fact that he was locked up there. With the arrival of each new prisoner, Rudolfo found himself painfully remembering his first few days. He had tried to talk to this new man, but the man did not seem to want to have anything to do with him. And now here he stood with a short piece of rope in his hands and a knotted piece of a sheet thrown around his neck like a noose.

Rudolfo quickly recalled one night not long ago when he'd gone out there with his razor. Suddenly he was face-to-face with a man who had gone out there with the same purpose in mind. And the reason just did not seem as right for anyone else as it had for him.

"Hey, friend, what's going on?" he asked with the most casual voice he could find at that moment. "You're not out here just to wash your face, are you?" He stared intently at the knotted noose.

"What's it to you?" the man spat back through clenched teeth.

"It's a great deal to me," Rudolfo answered. "I've stood right in this very room before, holding a razor to my own throat. I wasn't just getting ready to shave either! And I thought then that I had a mighty good reason for what I was about to do."

"And you think you've got the only one?" his friend asked. "If you only knew what I did, you'd understand why I don't want to live anymore."

"Then why don't you just tell me? Maybe I'll understand then. Come on, amigo, sit down. Let's talk."

"Leave me alone. What's my life to you? Let me go through with this."

"I'm sorry, friend, but I just can't let you do it. Now come on before I have to call the guards. Let's talk."

And so they did. Rudolfo had had a rough life and had done some seemingly unforgivable things, but as his new friend Cecilio began to tell his story, Rudolfo began to feel some of the hopeless despair that had brought him to the place where he stood with a noose around his neck.

"And after all of that," Cecilio continued, "I began to drink. Not just a little, but a lot. There have been times when I didn't even remember the night before, or the week before. I don't know why I felt I needed to drink. Does anyone really know why they do? I had a wonderfully sweet wife, four special sons, a good job, and close friends. But my drinking seemed to become one of the most important things in my life, and I slowly lost all my good friends. My boss told me one day I'd have to look for a job someplace else. Instead of all that sobering me up, it seemed to make me feel I had more excuses to do more drinking.

"One night after being out on one of my binges, I came home almost out of my mind drunk. My wife began to cry, as she often did. Our boys were all so upset. All five of them were crying and begging me to stop drinking. My loving wife tried to hold me and caress me and console me. As we often did when I was drunk, we began to fight. The boys must have sensed that this was a little more than just an argument, so they got in the middle of it too.

"'Papa, Papa, stop hitting our mama. Please don't. We love you. We love you, Papa. Papa, please don't fight. Stop it, stop it. You're hurting us. Oh, Papa, please.'

"I vaguely recall knocking my wife to the floor. And the last thing I remember was picking up my youngest son by the neck, and . . . and . . ."

And then Cecilio broke down. He couldn't talk anymore. He finally was able to tell Rudolfo that later that night, when he awoke from his drunken stupor, he found he had killed two of his sons before they could stop him. That's why he was in jail. And that's why he was standing in the toilet in the middle of the night with a noose around his neck.

Rudolfo spent most of that night talking with Cecilio. Before morning, Rudolfo had led Cecilio to find the peace he had sought for some time now, peace that passes all understanding. Thanks to the midnight prayers of Rudolfo, Cecilio was not a lonely outcast anymore. He gave his heart and life to the Lord. Rudolfo had not only gained a new friend, but he also had a new brother in the Lord.

12
A New Creation

As wonderful as it was to help his own family and friends to come to know the Lord, it did not take Rudolfo long to sense a need in his own life to grow in his personal relationship with his Saviour. Other letters to Olivia S. D. de Lerin included requests for some sort of additional Bible study help. Since he was such a new believer, he prayed for someone who might come and talk to him personally about his life and his growing relationship with the Lord. He had no idea who that someone might be; but if he was to grow in relationship with God, he needed some additional help.

Olivia S. D. de Lerin responded by putting him in touch with James Crane, a missionary who lived some hours away in Guadalajara. Missionary Crane had written a number of books and pamphlets, among which was a series of Bible studies which served as a correspondence course for personal one-on-one, at-home Bible studies. They were written to be used by people without much prior preparation or experience in studying the Bible. He had sent them to people all over Mexico, but this was the first time a request had come from a municipal jail.

The lessons were designed to be studied totally alone or with the supervision of a teacher. In the case of Rudolfo, James Crane would willingly serve as his correspondence teacher. That was the way James Crane was. Anyone who knew James Crane personally knew that this would give Rudolfo a definite advantage from the very beginning of his spiritual quest. James Crane had guided people in their Christian growth, as well as being one of the most active and respected church developers in the entire Mexico Mission group.

The lessons were simply designed. The student was to study the first one, answer the questions, do the homework, then send that lesson back to his teacher. James Crane would evaluate the responses, make some helpful comments, then send these along with the next lesson. In this way, there would be some communication, some evaluation, and, hopefully, a lot of Christian growth during his Bible studies.

Because of the tremendous work load he carried, James Crane seldom got personally involved in the lives of the people taking his course. In this case, it was his personal hope that from time to time he might be able to visit with Rudolfo personally. But that would have to come in God's good time. For now he just needed to send him the first lesson and wait for his reply.

Rudolfo could hardly believe it when he received the envelope and held the very first of the lessons in his hands. He could feel his heart pounding in his chest as he walked slowly back to the table in the corner of his cell. Before he opened the small manila envelope, he said a silent prayer that God would help him to learn, that He would help him to grow, and that He would help him to become all He needed and wanted him to be. He opened the package and began to read.

With the first lesson, Rudolfo also got some instructions about the use of it. The introductory material said:

> This workbook contains the materials for self-learning for spiritual growth of new brothers in Christ. Using fundamental teachings from the New Testament, the following themes will be studied: Security of Salvation, How to Grow in the Christian Life, The Believer's Home—The Local Church, The Holy Spirit—Our Helper, Liberty from the Power of Sin, Christian Baptism, and the Will of God in the Daily Life.

The first words of the first lesson spoke to him. "Dear One in Christ: Welcome to the family of faith. You can't imagine how great our joy is to have you as a new student in Christ." The Scripture study, based in part on Philippians 1:21, was

"For to me to live is Christ, and to die is gain."

Rudolfo knew at once that this kind of study was exactly what he had been needing. Now he could really learn more about the Lord in his life. Now he would be able to grow in Him in a personal and complete way. Just to think of those days not too long ago when he wanted to take his own life filled him with a sense of shame. Why would any man want to die? Especially at his own hand? And especially when there was so much to live for?

For the first time in a long time, Rudolfo didn't want to die. Even though that Scripture verse said it would be gain to do so . . . now. But now he wanted to live. He wanted to live in order to help others to come to know the saving faith and glorious life in Christ that he had experienced firsthand. He knew what it meant to believe in Christ and he wanted everyone else to have the same opportunity. If he were dead, he would not ever have that joy of seeing others come to know the Lord Who could save them from their sins, and at times, from themselves.

As the weeks went by, he worked his way through the lessons, faithfully reading the suggested readings in the Gospel of John and doing the homework suggested in the studies. The lessons not only included Scripture verses to read and memorize and apply to his life, but the challenging, thought-provoking questions caused him to think about all that the Scripture verses meant.

Almost every lesson included something to read, something to learn, and something to do. As much as he loved to read and to learn, it was that something to do which allowed him to reach out even more to those around him. He was instructed to "Give the five evangelistic tracts included with the lesson to five people who are not yet Christians." That was one of the easiest instructions he had been given. Almost everyone else in the entire prison fell into that category.

Another lesson asked him to read the tract "Let Me Have a Moment of Your Time," then send it in a letter to someone who was not a Christian. He also had a list of people like that. His own brothers and sisters needed to read that one!

He was encouraged to pray by name for some of the people who needed the Lord. He did not need a lot of encouragement to do something that for him seemed to be the right thing to do, but it was nice to know that God really wanted him to pray by name for other lost people.

The lessons all seemed so perfectly designed. They were so well written. And so personal! How could he ever thank the Lord enough for doing all that He was doing for him? And how could he ever thank James Crane for writing these wonderful lessons? And how could he ever thank Olivia S. D. de Lerin for directing them to him?

He didn't know. But by the time he finished the last lesson, he knew he was ready to unconditionally place his life at the disposition of the will of God. He knew something else too. He wanted to be baptized. He wanted to follow his Lord into the waters. He wanted to be a witness and example to others. And he wanted to be part of a local church. But how? It all seemed so impossible. Yet he knew something now that he did not know before—that with God nothing was impossible.

Rudolfo continued growing in the Lord. He could scarcely believe the changes in himself. At times he worried a little about how he had deceived God and his fellow human beings. He occasionally remembered those times when he thought it best to take his own life. He recalled how hateful he had been and how bitter and angry he was during those other years.

What a wonderful God he had, to be able to forgive him for all of that! What a caring and loving heavenly Father to be able to love him in spite of it all. What a marvelous *Re*-creator he had. He was the living, breathing, smiling, witnessing proof of that. There was very little left of that prideful, resentful, hateful, unforgiving "old" man. He had been made over now. He was truly a new creation!!

13

The Road to Penjamo

In February 1979 a surprising and wonderful thing happened in the lives of all the people involved in this story. They got together.

After all the letters that had gone back and forth from Penjamo to El Paso, Olivia S. D. de Lerin and her husband, Alfredo, wanted to have a personal visit with Rudolfo Halcon and his family. They were to be in Mexico for some other matters, so they arranged to take the cross-country bus from Mexico City, remembering from their other years in Mexico that the bus always went through Penjamo.

What they did not know was that because of a change in the road system, the bus now completely bypassed the little town. They did not realize it until it was almost too late to get off. They asked the bus driver to just let them off on the toll road that went around the town. For most people, that would have been something of a risk. For them, it would likely have been all right; but because of the driver's genuine concern for them, he refused their request.

They then asked that they be allowed to get off at the next town; but again, unknown to them, the bus had changed routes and no longer stopped at the next town either. With all the confusion, they decided to go on into Guadalajara where they could arrange with some friends there to help them get back to Penjamo the next day. So that's what they did.

Kay Weldon, missionary nurse and friend of the Lerins, got a call about 10:00 that night from the Guadalajara bus terminal. "*Hola.* Mrs. Lerin? Where are you? Of course you can stay overnight. I'm going to call Graciela to come with me. We'll be right there."

On the way to the station, Graciela recalled how her family and the Lerins had been such close friends when both had lived and worked some years ago in Saltillo. On the ride back to Kay's apartment, the Lerins told them all about the mix-up with the bus.

"But why do you need to get back to Penjamo so badly?" Kay asked them. From the way the Lerins looked at one another, Kay and Graciela thought the reason must be something of an important secret.

"*Es un secreto?*" Graciela asked.

"No," Alfredo Lerin answered. "It's not a secret, but it is important. We need to go back to Penjamo in order to visit someone special at the municipal jail."

That did it! It didn't take much for Kay to coax the rest of the story out of them. It was extremely exciting for them to hear about all that had been going on between them and Rudolfo. After a few phone calls to rearrange their work schedules, Kay and Graciela told them they'd be glad to drive them back to Penjamo the following day.

Early the next morning, they all piled into Kay's car and headed for Penjamo. The Lerins spent almost all the driving time telling them the entire story in detail. After all the months of writing to Rudolfo, the Lerins were thrilled at the prospect of finally getting to meet him face-to-face. Telling the story again made them all approach the visit with a renewed sense of excitement, anticipation, and a mixture of emotions. None of them really knew exactly what they'd find or how they would be received.

After three hours of driving, they arrived at the municipal jail only to hear some words that none of them had even thought about before. The uniformed guard on duty shocked them as he said, "I'm sorry, but today isn't visiting day at the jail. You'll have to come back tomorrow." That guard probably had trouble believing that this small group was for real.

Alfredo Lerin, as always, was dressed in suit and tie; and Olivia S. D. de Lerin, very properly dressed, was standing there between a young Mexican woman and a blonde American.

Alfredo made an emotional, but genuine, appeal. "Señor, we have come all the way from El Paso, Texas, to visit this man. We passed by on the bus last night; and after spending the night in Guadalajara, have driven back today for the express purpose of spending a few minutes with Rudolfo Halcon. Is there no way you can allow us to greet him? We won't take much of his time."

Something he said or did must have touched that sympathetic guard, for almost immediately he slowly nodded his head while saying, "OK, OK, you get special permission to visit today."

A sigh of relief escaped from each of the four people standing outside the gate. He led them right up to that door through which they had a clear view of the dusty courtyard on the other side.

Even though no one said anything about it, they were all thinking, That's the very place where the scrap-paper miracle first began. The guard's booming voice startled the small group of visitors as he suddenly called out, "Halcon, you got special visitors out here!"

It was one of those moments which can never be explained; for without a single word being spoken, the minute Rudolfo saw them, he seemed to know who they were. As the jailer opened the door, Rudolfo stood there with his arms outstretched toward the Lerins. With tears flowing down each of their faces, a group of people, who until moments before were only names on a written page, warmly greeted each other as *hermanos en Cristo* (brothers in the Lord)!

In her usual professional way, Olivia S. D. de Lerin began to present herself to Rudolfo: "I am Señora Olivia S. D. de ..." He did not need to know. He began calling them by name, saying he already knew who they were. Introductions from Kay and Graciela followed before the guard reminded them that even though this was a special visit, they had permission to accompany Rudolfo to his cell room. For a few minutes, they had all but forgotten they were standing there in the open door of the municipal jail of Penjamo. There was a lot of catching up to do that day. Even though Olivia and Rudolfo had been writing for some time, there were things each wanted to know about the other. At one point in their talk, Alfredo Lerin asked, "Rudolfo, how are you doing spiritually? Since you came to know the Lord, are there any people here with whom you can share? Do you read the Bible with any others? Is there at least one other person who is sympathetic to your Christianity?"

His answer surprised the whole group, for they were all expecting to hear him tell about his lonely spiritual walk.

"*Hermanos,* there are not only sympathizers here but good Christian friends," Rudolfo answered. "There are several who are already believers. And many more are listening to our message and are nearly ready to accept the Lord Jesus Christ as Saviour."

The visitors could hardly believe their ears. Broad smiles and incredulous looks passed from one to the other.

Rudolfo couldn't help but notice their expressions, but didn't know exactly what they meant. He continued, almost apologetically, "I hope I haven't done anything wrong. As a new Christian, I didn't know I was supposed to wait."

They assured him that he had done nothing wrong. Alfredo also asked if it would be all right to hold a brief service right there in his cell. Rudolfo was thrilled.

"Oh, *sí, hermanos.* There is such an interest, and I am so new in all of this and do not know what all to do and say. I know so little, and the men are always ready to learn more. But first, could we just talk some more?"

He was like a man hungry to hear, wanting to learn, desiring to know more. It seemed to those who were there that day that they were sitting in a jail cell of many years ago listening to Paul or Silas. They went on talking about basic spiritual growth, things that most people take for granted—things like prayer and reading the Bible and sharing his faith, things he'd already been doing a lot even without knowing how. They talked about the church and the meaning of it.

Alfredo told him, "You already have a church right here. You don't have a building or a preacher or baptisms, but you have a church. No, you *are* a church." There sat a wise old seminary professor, giving a lecture to his one-person class. But there was never another one like it.

Rudolfo was interested in what Kay and Graciela did. Graciela told him about the First Baptist Church of Guadalajara, where her brother was the pastor and where she sang in the choir. They told him about Sunday School and missions that were going on all around their part of the country.

Kay told him about the hospital and how she came to be working there now. They tried to assure him that their church and their fellow missionaries would be praying for him in the future. Little did he know how much that very church and that very group of missionaries would mean to him and his family in the years to come. No one thought that his family would be baptized into the First Baptist Church of Guadalajara some years later.

In order not to abuse this special visiting time, Alfredo Lerin asked again about the possibility of leading a brief worship service there. Rudolfo wanted him to lead one, not only for the sake of their hearing the gospel again, but he wanted his prison friends and brothers to know his friends and brothers in the Lord from El Paso and Guadalajara. He wanted them to know about this small group of people who were genuinely interested in them, so he began to call them in. Of course, during the course of the visit in his room, they had already attracted quite a group of curious onlookers.

After about seven or eight other men arrived, these brothers in the Lord gave brief testimonies of their new life in Christ. Most of them did not have Bibles of their own, so the visitors told them they would get some for them at a later time. Kay, Graciela, and the Lerins had arrived at the prison with their own hymnals, as most Mexican Christians are in the habit of doing, since the church does not supply them like they do in the States. They sang two or three hymns, attracting a crowd of people to the door which was opened onto the patio. Alfredo read some Scripture passages and preached a brief message. Kay prayed. And then it was time for the small group of visitors to leave.

Before the other men left the room, each of them was assured of the thoughts and prayers that this group of visitors would carry with them. The use of the term *hermano* was something very special for the visitors and for the men. Out of respect for their new friend and brother Rudolfo, the other prisoners left the room to give him a few moments alone with his special visitors. Most of them had never known the guards to allow anyone from the outside to enter a cell on a day other than visiting day.

In the typically formal Latin way, Olivia asked, "As this special afternoon is drawing to a close, I have a request of you. If it would not be an inconvenience, we would so like to visit with your family today. Would that be all right with you? And with them?"

"Oh, Señora Lerin, that pleases me very much. And I know my family would be honored to meet you." Dropping his head very close to his chest and lowering his voice more than he had all day, he said, "But in all honesty, I fear you will not find the living conditions to be very pleasant or comfortable. But if you want, I will give you directions to find the place where they are living."

"Where they are living doesn't matter to us at all. Please, tell us how to find them."

After he was sure they knew how to find the abandoned house where Socorro and the children were living, he walked them toward the front gate. It did not matter that most of the other prisoners were watching them as they spoke their final words. In all his eloquence, he wanted to thank them for coming. He thanked Kay and Graciela for their part in helping get the Lerins back there. He was overcome with humility for all it had meant to him to finally see these people, to touch them, to sing and pray with them, just to be there in their very presence. Interesting, but that's exactly the way each person in that small group felt about him at that very moment.

14
That We Might Learn

After leaving the jail, they went in search of the family. Even though he had referred to where they lived as a house, and given them the address, they drove by the location several times before stopping, for the place did not seem to be a home at all. It was a large, old, very run-down building that from the street appeared to be totally abandoned. There was no sign that anyone lived there now or had lived there for some time.

It was the kind of place that should have had a sign on the front door that said Condemned. In truth, it had been officially condemned some time before. Kay parked the car at the curb, self-consciously aware that it was the only vehicle in sight.

As they got out of the car, they noticed several of the neighbors suspiciously looking them over. No one spoke. They did not take time to voice their thoughts. There were other things on their minds. They walked up to where a concrete block substituted for a step, and Alfredo Lerin stepped up and knocked at the large wooden door.

There was a hollow echo behind the door, as it rattled on its large rusty hinges. He might have looked through the windows, except that where there had been windows before, there were now stacks of bricks, rocks, and blocks, all concreted over to cover the opening. As they stood there, hands full of fruits and vegetables they had just purchased at the market, they were all but convinced that they had arrived at the wrong place. Then they heard sounds of someone coming to the door.

A large chain was being removed from its place on the other side before the door opened slightly, and a little girl with big brown eyes and a slightly dirty face timidly peeked through the opening. She looked directly at each one of the group. When her eyes finally got around to Olivia S. D. de Lerin, she bent down so she would be on the same eye level as the little girl. With her kind and gentle voice, she asked the little girl, "Is there a Mrs. Halcon here?"

Without securing the door again, the little girl backed away from it without responding in any way. She did not even bother to say a word. As the door remained slightly open, they remained standing outside and waited without saying anything, although it's probable that each one of them felt their hearts in their throats as they tried to anticipate what was going to happen next.

In a few minutes, a somewhat older girl came to the door. Again Olivia asked her question, "Is there a Mrs. Halcon here?" To which she answered, "Sí."

"Could we speak with her, please?"

Without saying anything more, this young lady opened the door wide enough for them to enter and motioned for them to enter a large open entranceway. What used to be a beautiful place was now a shambles. Just ahead was a typical open patio area. At other times, it too had been filled with flowers, but now there was nothing but weeds. The last traces of a wall-clinging bougainvillea fought to grow in that weed-infested ground. What at one time had been head-high poinsettias were now only rustling stalks scraping along the walls.

A quick glance revealed a series of rooms with doors and windows that had at one time opened all around the spacious, tiled patio, but now were boarded shut. It was truly a depressing sight.

The older girl led them to the one open door near the back of the patio. A woman appeared there, holding the hand of the first little girl who had answered the door. Immediately, the older girl ran to her sister's side. The visitors could tell that all of the family were somewhat apprehensive about their being there.

Olivia S. D. de Lerin stepped forward and simply said, "Socorro?" The woman nodded. "I am Olivia S. D. de Lerin, and we've come all the way from El Paso just to meet you and your family."

Socorro ran to her and threw herself into her arms. With embraces, kisses, and tears, any fears any of them had were quickly dismissed.

"Oh, Señora, I've waited so long to meet you. I've read your name so many times. God has truly answered one of my prayers. Children, come here. Do not be afraid. I want you to meet that wonderful woman whose letters gave your father such hope when he didn't seem to have any other place to turn."

Two young boys emerged from the open door, and all the children eagerly ran to greet the Lerins. The silent, sad faces of the two little girls rapidly changed to happy, active faces like those of any little girls anyplace in the world.

Quickly, Kay and Graciela were introduced to all of them as well. And like the Lerins, they too were warmly welcomed by Rudolfo, Jr., Socorro, Ruth, and Daniel. They were polite enough, but like most children in the presence of strangers, after the initial greetings, they kept a safe distance.

The fruit had been brought as a gift; so as the visitors held out their hands full of fresh red apples, green-colored oranges, bright yellow bananas, and pinkish-looking mangoes, the children just could not stay away any longer. Waiting for an approving nod from Soccoro, they came to take the fruit and immediately began to taste it with their eyes right there in the patio. They hadn't had such an abundance of fresh fruit in a long time.

It was all just as Rudolfo had said. Socorro really was glad to see them, all of them. For some minutes everyone stood there talking outside of that room. Socorro was obviously embarrassed about their living conditions as she said, "It's so cold inside. Let's just visit out here. Children, take the fruit into the kitchen and bring the chairs out here."

They scurried into the house, already talking about what piece of the fruit they were going to eat first. They returned almost immediately with two straight-backed chairs. These were the only chairs they had, although the visitors had no way of knowing that. Along with the chairs, the boys brought out a variety of boxes and crates for everyone else. The Lerins took the chairs, while Kay, Graciela, Socorro, and the older children sat on the boxes.

Socorro did most of the talking that afternoon, which is exactly what the Lerins wanted her to do. They wanted to learn as much as they could about all of them; it might be a long time before they'd get back to see them again. They wanted to hear about everything that had been going on in her life. As she talked that day, she never complained. She did express her fear of the authorities. She admitted that with each knock at the door, she was afraid it might be the authorities asking them to vacate their place in that old condemned house. It wasn't much, but it was the only place they had to live right now, so she had reason to be afraid.

"I'm still working as a maid," she continued, "but for another family now. The other people I worked for wanted me to work full time, but I chose not to. Now I only work mornings. We could have used the extra money, but I wanted to be here with the children when they came home from school. It's a sacrifice, but only a small one to pay, for I think they need love as a family too." Her voice choked slightly as she looked at each of her children before continuing.

"At the beginning, right after we lost our house and all, all we had left was each other and that feeling of love that held us all together."

Rudolfo, Jr., picked up the conversation. "I have a job too. It's not much. I spend some time each day running errands for another family. I wash their cars, sweep their sidewalks, things like that. The thing that makes me happy is that I can help support my family right now. Every afternoon after my classes, I go to the jail. They've given me permission to visit freely there because I'm helping Papa with all the craft projects. Papa's a good teacher and he's helping the other prisoners learn how to weave."

Socorro was now able to speak again. "Rudolfo was always good with his hands. He never thought of it as any kind of art. It was just what he had been taught to do. They're letting the prisoners sell their work now."

And Rudolfo, Jr., said with pride, "I'm the contact person for selling all the products they make. So you see I'm learning to be a businessman too. My mother tells me that beside all that, I'm also learning a very valuable trade while I'm learning a very valuable lesson."

"Sometimes it's hard for young people today," Socorro added, "but my son is learning to help others, even though his very own family needs so much help themselves." She reached over and gave him a motherly hug.

Before the day was over, Socorro allowed the visitors to see their "house." It was nothing to describe. It had a small sitting room where the children studied and played, a small kitchen area off to one side, and a bedroom with only one bed. If anyone wondered where they all slept, no one needed to ask. One of the rooms had its own skylight, for there was a large hole that looked right out at the sky.

As she led them through the rooms, she told them about the Gideon New Testament. She didn't know it, but she and the children would soon be receiving Bibles of their very own. Olivia S. D. de Lerin also told the children about Sunday School and encouraged them to look for someplace where they could study the Bible. She told them she would be sending them some material they could study at home if they would like to receive it.

"Oh, sí, Señora. What will it be like? Will it be something like catechism?"

"Not exactly. You'll see when it comes," she responded.

Almost as a group, Kay, Graciela, and the Lerins tried to express how sorry they were for all that happened to the Halcon family. In response to that, Socorro simply said, "Thank you for being concerned. But it's all right. It's like my favorite verse, Psalm 119:71, says, " 'It is good for me that I have been afflicted; that I might learn thy statutes.' " She believed it too. And she preached that editorial writer, that seminary professor, that missionary nurse, and that active church member a very good sermon that day! How they must have wished that all might be so sensitive to God, that they too might learn!

They assured her, as they had her husband, that they would seek out others from other churches, other people in other cities, to help them personally. They had already talked about a mission church and again expressed hope that there might be the possibility of establishing one there. The family was assured that they would be praying for them wherever they were. They would never be forgotten. Kay Weldon gave her word that afternoon.

Every Monday afternoon the missionaries in the city of Guadalajara gathered in one of their homes for a time of sharing and praying. The Monday following that trip, Kay honored that promise to lift them up to the Lord as she shared something of that scrap-paper miracle, concluding with her visit to the jail.

Sure enough, God had been working through Olivia S. D. de Lerin and James Crane and others. His Spirit had led Pastor Octavio Gaspar and the First Baptist Church of Guadalajara to begin sending some of its members to Penjamo every weekend. The group that went from Guadalajara took the cross-country early morning bus in order that they could be there early on Sunday morning to meet and minister to the prisoners and their families.

It was not the first time this church had reached out to prisoners. They had been ministering to men and women in the prison in Guadalajara for some time. The leadership of the church was very familiar with the distinct problems prisoners faced; so Bible studies were begun both inside the prison and outside of it. First Baptist Church extended its ministry and rented a small house near the prison, where they held Sunday School and worship services. They also allowed Socorro and the children to live there during the week. What an unusual blessing of the Lord for the family, the prisoners, and for those who went to hear them tell it.

As time went on, the entire family came to Guadalajara to be baptized and became members of the First Baptist Church.

15
My Grace Is Sufficient

One of the genuine concerns expressed by almost everyone involved in the story of the scrap-paper miracle was for some kind of legal help for this new friend and brother in the Lord. He had been without help for too long. Of course, everyone knew that he was willing to suffer more time there, if that was what his Lord required of him; but still, everyone was concerned for him.

He tried to get permission to represent himself, but it did not seem to be possible to do much on his own behalf. Besides, considering the reason behind his arrest (legal fraud), the officials would probably not have believed too much of what he would have said anyway.

Some of the church people in Guadalajara did get in touch with a Christian lawyer with the hope that he might be able to help somehow. Everyone knew that Rudolfo would likely have to serve some time; but everyone also knew that he might be there a lot longer than he had already served, without some professional help.

As with everything else that had happened in this case, it took several extra months for the Guadalajara lawyer to get official permission to visit him as a lawyer. Part of that waiting time was spent trying to put together all the facts, in order that he might better represent him.

When he had all the information he needed, he arranged to

make the trip to Penjamo to talk with his new client. Their first meeting was a tense one. Surprisingly, he found Rudolfo at first unwilling to open up to him. Rudolfo said, "Yes, I am a professing Christian now, totally forgiven by God for what I have done, but I can't totally forgive myself. I find myself coming face-to-face with a sense of personal shame every new day, especially when I think of my former life."

The lawyer tried to reassure him by saying, "I really haven't come here to dig into your former life, except for those certain facts that I have to know in order to help you." During succeeding visits, they established a good friendship, and Rudolfo found himself overjoyed to have a new friend to talk with, especially someone who was finally trying to represent him in the courts of Mexico.

Following the visits with the lawyer, Rudolfo felt quite sure he would soon be brought to trial. At least something would happen. This Christian lawyer became something like a counselor to Rudolfo. He was someone with whom he could share thoughts and feelings he had never shared with anyone else. During one of the lawyer's visits, he talked about some very serious problems.

"Had it not been for the kind goodness of the Lord, I could not have endured the interminable waiting and the continuing pressure of prison life. Even in the face of this renewed hope, I had long periods of intense depression that sent me reeling downward to what seemed to be the very bottom of my spirit. It seemed during those times that there was a feeling of overpowering sadness all around me. There was a desperate kind of searching and longing for something unknown.

"I felt so separated from God, and there was even a sense of loneliness from my own family. It was something I couldn't put into words. It was a feeling that only a person who has had to spend a lot of time locked up in a jail could fully understand."

Even though his lawyer had never been locked up as a prisoner, he tried to listen to his new client as a Christian person who needed someone to hear him, as well as a man who needed his legal advice.

In spite of all the frustrations and doubts, Rudolfo continued to read his Bible faithfully, for he knew that God's grace was sufficient. Just as he had at one time read and reread the words, "Be thou faithful unto death," he now read, reread, prayed, and thought about God and His grace. He used the words as a mental fortress to break down those moments of despair and distress. Almost subconsciously he found himself repeating those words, "My grace is sufficient. My grace is sufficient."

His Bible study time was another of the things that sustained him when all else seemed to be taking a toll on his spirit. Whereas a weaker person might have allowed such adverse circumstances to come between him and the necessity of reading the Bible, Rudolfo knew that without this significant practice in his life he would spiritually dry up and die. He needed the power that was gained by constant contact with the Bible. He studied it now with an ever greater intensity. He not only wanted to read it, he wanted to apply it to his life in an in-depth way.

James Crane had given his study book an appropriate title. It was a title that left no doubt as to what these studies would attempt to accomplish in one's life. It left no doubt Who the One was Who would help in the accomplishment. The book was called *My Growth in Christ.*

As he immersed himself in the studies, Rudolfo felt sure he could almost measure his spiritual growth each day. Whether others could see the difference in his life or not was not the most important thing at the moment. What he wanted to do right now was to establish a growing relationship with God.

How he wanted to be a greater witness to others for His Lord! He seriously tried to apply that chapter that spoke of "The Christian Walk." He wanted to walk in new life and by faith and not by sight. He wanted to walk in the spirit. And when Paul, himself a prisoner, wrote in Ephesians 4:1, "I therefore, the prisoner of the Lord, beseech you that ye walk worthy of the vocation wherewith ye are called, with all lowliness and meekness, with longsuffering, forbearing one another in love; endeavouring to keep the unity of the Spirit in the bond of peace," it was almost more than he could comprehend. He was reminded to walk in love. He was encouraged to walk worthy of the Lord, "being fruitful in every good work, and increasing in the knowledge of God."

That was what he so wanted to do. But there were times when it was hard. Not everyone understood his newfound spiritual life. Not everyone wanted to listen. But 2 Peter 3:11 reminded him of the kind of person he should be in all conversation. The Bible never promised that everyone would understand him. It never said that all men would want to listen to him.

It was pretty clearly written, however, that he was supposed to keep on telling people about Jesus, the difference He had made in him, and the difference He was willing to make in the lives of others. He never really questioned God outright; he had some trouble totally understanding why God made him stay here, but he knew more about the kind of life he was to live while he was there. Abiding in Christ, walking in truth, and guarding His commandments—these were not easy things to do, but at no place in his Bible studies had he ever read that the Christian life was supposed to be easy.

He applied for home correspondence seminary studies. The Mexican Baptist Seminary in Mexico City provided these for him. He never presumed that he would graduate with a degree, but he wanted to use every available resource in order to better his life. He spent hours reading, studying, writing, learning, and waiting. While he waited, he prayed. And prayed some more.

His prayers had changed as much as his life. But then again, wasn't that what Christian growth was supposed to be about?

His prayers used to be prayers of bitterness, desperation, petition, filled with personal needs he thought God was supposed to take care of in his life. Now he prayed more like this:

> Dear Loving and Kind Heavenly Father: I thank You for the way You have cared for me. I thank You for the way You have shown Your love to me. I thank You for listening to me in my times of distress and frustration. I thank You for waiting for me during those times in my life

My Grace Is Sufficient 77

when I didn't so readily come seeking You there. I have something special to ask You, loving Father. Dear Lord, I ask You to help me. I have a genuine desire in my heart to be used in an even greater way. I don't know what that way is. But, Father, let it be Your way. I've never thought about the hurting people who are locked away behind bars. Maybe You could use me in the future to minister to them. I've heard some talk about people called chaplains who work with such people. If that is Your will for my life, show me how to attain it. I will try to simply rest in Your decisions for me, waiting patiently for You, knowing that You want to give me the desires of my heart. You know, dear God, that I do not wish for You to do any of these things for me simply because it is my personal desire. Do for me that which You do, when in Your timing, You are ready for me to take that step in my life. And I will continue to praise You and honor You and thank You. Keep me faithful to You. Amen.

Epilogue—What's Happened Since

I could end this story just about there, but I think there are some unfinished details you might like to know. What happened to Rudolfo Halcon? Is he still in the Penjamo jail? And what about his family?

I've already told you in the preface that the first I heard about Rudolfo Halcon and his story was during a missionary prayer meeting in Guadalajara in 1979. When Kay Weldon first told us this story, we were all fascinated and deeply moved. I remember saying right after she told us, "Is someone else going to write this story down? If not, I want to." Whether they thought I was serious or not, no one indicated an interest in doing so. So I did!

Later that same year, I fell in love with Kay Weldon and asked her to marry me. She accepted. She resigned her appointment, following which we lived in the States before going back to Guadalajara in 1981 for joint volunteer work at that same Mission hospital where she had served for many years. God used those months in my life in a special way, following which I responded to His call to serve as a missionary chaplain. We had to return to the States to continue my studies and preparations. On our driving trip out of Mexico, we chose a route that would take us directly to Penjamo, so we could visit that little jail. We misjudged the road in, so we took a small driving tour of the city before locating the central plaza. Having never been there before, but having heard about it all for several years, I had a pretty exact mental image of what it would be like. The plaza was almost exactly as I thought it would be. There were the benches and the flowers and the bandstand in the middle. And there were the trees, their branches intertwined together to form a ceiling of green.

The birds were singing for us, just as they had so many times for Rudolfo. And there were the people—old men, young children, lovers, shoeshine boys. Beautiful curved arches supported by concrete pillars framed the front walk of the jail. By just walking a few more steps, we crossed the street and found ourselves under the portico that shaded that side of the street.

Then suddenly we were there. We stood outside the large door that looked out onto the street at the same time it looked into the courtyard of the jail. Brown-uniformed guards stood all around the door. Some of them sat just inside the room. We were there just outside the jail where all those letters had been written and sent. How my heart pounded at the thought of it. Postmark: Penjamo Jail.

Kay identified us and asked if we could visit Señor Halcon. He must have heard her, for by the time the gate was opened, he was standing there with arms outstretched, waiting for us to enter.

There were quick introductions and Mexican hugs from everyone. There were broad smiles and quick tears and a lot of talk. Oh, how I wanted so to understand exactly what was being said; but try as I may, I could not follow every thought. (And I thought I could understand everything in Spanish!) I did understand enough to know how glad he was to see us. Many times his letters had included phrases like, "Although I do not personally know your husband, I feel I know him spiritually, and I hope someday to have the privilege of stretching out my hands to him and welcoming him to this special little corner of my cell." That day he had that opportunity when he invited us to accompany him into his cell.

It was more like a small room than a cell. There was a cot in each corner, separated by small tables. On his table sat that very typewriter on which all those letters had been written.

And hanging behind his bed was a handmade sign that read, "Be thou faithful unto death." One large nail was stuck in the wall above the bed with several hangers of pants and shirts on it. A stack of tortillas and a pot of meat broth sat at the end of the bed. There was one small chair at each table; he quickly pulled them up for us to use. He sat on the edge of his bed, that same bed where he'd thought about suicide.

For what seemed like a long time, we sat there talking, old friends now. From time to time, he would call someone else into the room and present them to us. And in almost every case, he would call them brother, indicating that they too had made a profession of faith and were part of the family of believers.

Most of them had come to know the Lord due to the witness of the man with whom we were sitting and talking. As I met them, I wondered if these were some of the 11 men he had written us about who had been praying each day from 5:00 until 7:00 A.M. for the spiritual release of other people who were "prisoners of a different kind, bound in the chains of Satan's sin." It wasn't important. Even though they remained prisoners in this jail, each of them had attained that spiritual liberty in their souls.

The words flowed from him in abundant beauty. Even though I missed the exact meaning of all he said, I could tell by his tone of voice and his way of expressing himself that he was speaking from the very bottom of his heart. Later Kay filled me in on the parts of the conversation that I didn't understand.

He told us of his dream to be used of God someday in a special way. He asked us to pray for God's will to be done regarding his trial and release. He was willing to stay there if it meant he could witness to more and more people. He asked us to pray for his family. He told us where they lived and hoped we'd go by before we left town that day.

One of the last things he told us to do was to thank all those people who had faithfully prayed for him during his years in jail. We told him we would be going back to the States soon and would likely not see him again before we left.

He wanted us to be sure to thank all the people who had remembered him to God. He wanted us to express to them his gratitude and let them know that through their prayers God had given his life back to him and saved him from his sin.

Many of the people had likely prayed something like, "Bless all the lost people who need You," without ever praying for him by name. His plea to us was that we tell people over and over and over that they should not stop praying for the lost people of the world. We assured him that wherever we spoke we would repeat his message.

As we were leaving, he gave us some of the handmade craft items he and the other prisoners were selling. We tried to pay him for them, but he wouldn't hear of it. We still use that plastic-weave basket as a prayer reminder of a man whose life continues to be a witness through the lives of the many people he helped lead to the Lord.

And then it was time to go, although we didn't really want to leave. We hugged, cried, and prayed. And we left him at the gate, where he remained standing for as long as we could see him. We looked back and waved, then walked on in silence around the corner where our car was parked. Only after we got into the car did either of us speak. It was one of those special moments when we really didn't know what to say. And we didn't want to break that feeling immediately.

We visited the family after that and saw the house that they were using for Bible studies and church worship. We rejoiced with all of them, and they with us; for when they had heard Kay was marrying and leaving the country, they thought they'd never have the opportunity to greet her again, and certainly never thought they'd ever meet her husband.

It was a wonderful day. After we made a circle and joined hands around that room, one of them led in prayer. I could feel the strong grip of the hands on either side of me. I could hear the emotion-filled voice as it worded the prayer. I could not see the faces. I could only count the pairs of feet. Even that was difficult. My tears of joy and excitement flowed freely. We were standing there all right, standing on holy ground. And I knew it!

Over the following years we lost contact with the Halcons. In one of the last letters written to Kay's mother, whose prayer group was always writing to encourage him, Rudolfo wrote some exciting news. Unfortunately, his emotional and flowery manner of expressing himself do not translate as well as I would like; but in brief he said:

> My heart and life are full of joy at this moment. It's a joy so complete that I don't have the words to properly express it to you. My blessed Lord Jesus has manifested himself for the second time in my life. He has opened the doors of this prison. One month and 15 days ago, my Saviour freed me. There are many people who have told me that miracles don't exist anymore; nevertheless, with the passing of time, our Lord and Saviour Jesus Christ has manifested Himself in all His power. Please share this happiness with all those who have been praying for me.

His release from jail had come almost eight years after he had been arrested. It didn't take an expert to know that with that kind of jail record, it was going to be difficult to get a full-time job.

So, he returned to the only honest work he had known—woodwork, carpentry. He was good with his hands. And he still liked to work with wood. Besides, it allowed him to gain back some of the self-respect he had lost during his years in jail. It had not all ended up exactly as he thought it would; but it was good, honest, and it was what God had given him to do.

One thing is certain. Only God in His mighty and mysterious way of working could have brought together the multiple ministries of the Baptist Spanish Publishing House, Gideons International, a Baptist hospital in Guadalajara, a missionary nurse who worked there, a missionary writer, two Mexican Baptist churches, a Baptist Women prayer group in New Mexico, a volunteer student worker soon to be a hospital chaplain, and all of you, who bathed it so generously in prayer.

Even though Rudolfo Halcon was a changed man with a distinct difference in his life after prison, it was extremely difficult for him to continue with his life in the way he wanted to. Society, former friends, and former enemies treated him differently now. He was all but forced to assume another name, begin another identity, and move to another place. It may not have been the exact way to begin again, but apparently it worked for him. Even I could not locate him some months ago when I was trying to update the story to the present.

As you may have guessed by now, all of this has also made a difference in my life. Since I've been serving here as a missionary chaplain, it has been a driving and forceful reminder that I must always be available to God, helping to meet whatever needs of whatever people He sends my way. Thank you for the multiple ways you support us, most of all through your constant prayers.

Allow me to reemphasize the request that Rudolfo made to so many people during his time in jail. He was a great letter writer and continued writing to anyone who would take the time to write him back. As I've said, Kay's mother was active in her prayer group in New Mexico, and they wrote him expressing their prayer support for him. He told them the same thing about the personal results he felt due to their prayers on his behalf.

I think that is perhaps one of the significant points in all of this—that people all over the world are receiving prayer benefits from Christian people who are lifting up unknown and unseen needs. Many of those people need to know the Lord. Many of them need to boldly speak to those all around them of the power of the Lord which they know is available. Many may be living in economic depression or family difficulties which they cope with every day. Many are lonely or have sick children. Many of the breadwinners are out of work. Many try to keep their families going while they are the only parent their children know.

But I want to be faithful to my promise. Whoever you are, and wherever you are, remember there are people waiting for your prayers. There are people waiting for God to touch their lives. You may never know their names. You may never receive word on this earth that your prayers have been answered; but pray. Keep praying without ceasing. Lift up the lost and hurting people of this world.

And in your prayers, I beg you to remember my friend Rudolfo Halcon. Pray for his wife, Socorro; and for his children, Rudolfo, Jr.; Socorro; Ruth; and Daniel. As you bring them to mind, let them be constant reminders of God's love, joy, peace, grace, and faithfulness to us.

And may we never forget the message of that scrap-paper miracle, that we are to be faithful in our service to Him, "faithful unto death." May it be so in your life and in mine. Amen. And Amen.

About the author

Don Madaris, a native Alabamian, is a musician, a composer, a writer, and a teacher. He has sung with Fred Waring's Pennsylvanians, the Home Mission Board's Spring Street Singers, and the Broadman Singers.

While serving with the Tennessee Baptist Convention's music and recreation departments, he composed the first senior adult musical, *Count on Us!*, and the first single adult musical, *Touch Life*. He has written several religious dramas and is the author of a memory book entitled *Little Donald Lee, Miss Etta G., and the Two-Room Schoolhouse*.

He and his wife, Kay, have served as Foreign Mission Board representatives in Mexico for the last ten years.